North Carolina Sentencing Handbook

with Felony, Misdemeanor, and DWI Sentencing Grids

James M. Markham
Shea Riggsbee Denning

UNC

**SCHOOL OF
GOVERNMENT**

The School of Government at the University of North Carolina at Chapel Hill works to improve the lives of North Carolinians by engaging in practical scholarship that helps public officials and citizens understand and improve state and local government. Established in 1931 as the Institute of Government, the School provides educational, advisory, and research services for state and local governments. The School of Government is also home to a nationally ranked Master of Public Administration program, the North Carolina Judicial College, and specialized centers focused on community and economic development, information technology, and environmental finance.

As the largest university-based local government training, advisory, and research organization in the United States, the School of Government offers up to 200 courses, webinars, and specialized conferences for more than 12,000 public officials each year. In addition, faculty members annually publish approximately 50 books, manuals, reports, articles, bulletins, and other print and online content related to state and local government. The School also produces the *Daily Bulletin Online* each day the General Assembly is in session, reporting on activities for members of the legislature and others who need to follow the course of legislation.

Operating support for the School of Government's programs and activities comes from many sources, including state appropriations, local government membership dues, private contributions, publication sales, course fees, and service contracts.

Visit sog.unc.edu or call 919.966.5381 for more information on the School's courses, publications, programs, and services.

Michael R. Smith, DEAN
Thomas H. Thornburg, SENIOR ASSOCIATE DEAN
Jen Willis, ASSOCIATE DEAN FOR DEVELOPMENT
Michael Vollmer, ASSOCIATE DEAN FOR ADMINISTRATION

FACULTY

Whitney Afonso	Norma Houston	Kimberly L. Nelson
Trey Allen	Cheryl Daniels Howell	David W. Owens
Gregory S. Allison	Jeffrey A. Hughes	William C. Rivenbark
David N. Ammons	Willow S. Jacobson	Dale J. Roenigk
Ann M. Anderson	Robert P. Joyce	John Rubin
Maureen Berner	Diane M. Juffras	Jessica Smith
Mark F. Botts	Dona G. Lewandowski	Meredith Smith
Anita R. Brown-Graham	Adam Lovelady	Carl W. Stenberg III
Peg Carlson	James M. Markham	John B. Stephens
Leisha DeHart-Davis	Christopher B. McLaughlin	Charles Szypszak
Shea Riggsbee Denning	Kara A. Millonzi	Shannon H. Tufts
Sara DePasquale	Jill D. Moore	Aimee N. Wall
James C. Drennan	Jonathan Q. Morgan	Jeffrey B. Welty
Richard D. Ducker	Ricardo S. Morse	Richard B. Whisnant
Jacquelyn Greene	C. Tyler Mulligan	

CONTENTS

Felony Sentencing

1 Determine the Applicable Law

Choose the appropriate sentencing grid based on the defendant's date of offense.

> Offenses committed on or after October 1, 2013

> Offenses committed December 1, 2011–September 30, 2013

> Offenses committed December 1, 2009–November 30, 2011

> Offenses committed December 1, 1995–November 30, 2009

> Offenses committed October 1, 1994–November 30, 1995

Notes

Grid applicability. The defendant must be sentenced under the law that existed at the time of his or her offense. State v. Whitehead, 365 N.C. 444 (2012). Subsequent changes to the grid should not be retroactively applied. State v. Lee, 228 N.C. App. 324 (2013).

Range of offense dates. If the precise offense date is unknown and the range of possible dates crosses an effective date threshold, use the law most favorable to the defendant. State v. Poston, 162 N.C. App. 642 (2004). If a continuing offense occurred over a range of dates, use the law in place when the offense was completed. State v. Mullaney, 129 N.C. App. 506 (1998).

Older offenses. Offenses committed before October 1, 1994, are sentenced under the Fair Sentencing Act or other prior law.

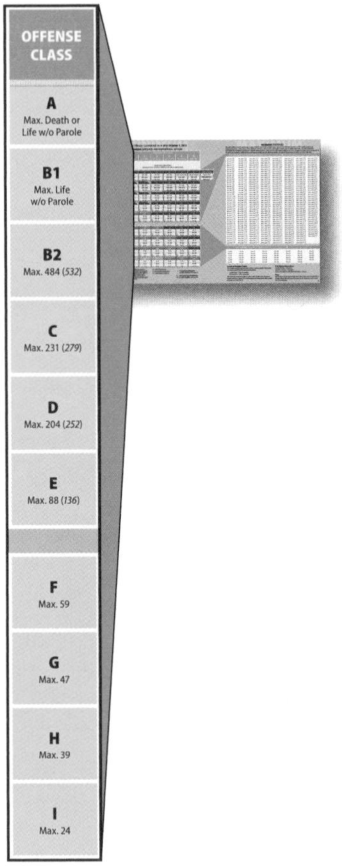

2 Determine the Offense Class

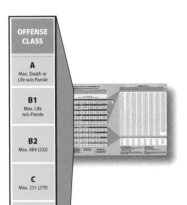

North Carolina felonies are assigned to one of ten offense classes—Class A through Class I, from most to least serious. Identify the offense class of the crime being sentenced. See **APPENDIX A**, Offense Class Table for Felonies.

Offense Class Reductions

Unless otherwise provided by law, the following step-down rules apply for attempts, conspiracies, and solicitations to commit a felony and for other participants in crimes.

Offense Class Reductions										
Principal Offense	**A**	**B1**	**B2**	**C**	**D**	**E**	**F**	**G**	**H**	**I**
Same classification as principal: Aiding and Abetting Accessory before the Fact (G.S. 14-5.2)	A	B1	B2	C	D	E	F	G	H	I
One classification lower: Attempt (G.S. 14-2.5) Conspiracy (G.S. 14-2.4)	B2	B2	C	D	E	F	G	H	I	Class 1 Misd.
Two classifications lower: Solicitation (G.S. 14-2.6) Accessory after the Fact (G.S. 14-7)	C	C	D	E	F	G	H	I	Class 1 Misd.	Class 2 Misd.

Offense class sidebar:

OFFENSE CLASS
A Max. Death or Life w/o Parole
B1 Max. Life w/o Parole
B2 Max. 484 (532)
C Max. 231 (279)
D Max. 204 (252)
E Max. 88 (136)
F Max. 59
G Max. 47
H Max. 39
I Max. 24

Offense Class Enhancements

With appropriate factual findings, the offense class of certain felonies may be increased under the enhancements set out in the table below.

Offense Class Enhancements

Habitual Felon (G.S. 14-7.6)	Offenses committed on/after 12/1/2011—Four-class enhancement, capped at Class C (unless already Class A, B1, or B2) Offenses committed before 12/1/2011—Enhance to Class C (unless already Class A, B1, or B2)
Habitual Breaking and Entering (G.S. 14-7.31)	Offenses committed on/after 12/1/2011—Enhance to Class E
Armed Habitual Felon (G.S. 14-7.41)	Offenses committed on/after 10/1/2013—Enhance to Class C, with 120-month mandatory minimum sentence
Bullet-Proof Vest Enhancement (G.S. 15A-1340.16C)	Offenses committed on/after 12/1/1999—One-class enhancement
Gang Activity (G.S. 15A-1340.16E(a))	Offenses committed on/after 12/1/2017—One-class enhancement, capped at Class C
Gang Leader or Organizer (G.S. 15A-1340.16E(b))	Offenses committed on/after 12/1/2017—Two-class enhancement, capped at Class C
Protective Order Violation (G.S. 50B-4.1(d))	Offenses committed on/after 3/1/2002—One-class enhancement
Injury to Pregnant Woman (G.S. 14-18.2(b))	*Repealed* for offenses committed on/after 12/1/2011—One-class enhancement

3 Calculate the Prior Record Level

The defendant is assigned to one of six prior record levels (I through VI) according to a point scale based on his or her criminal history.

Points for Prior Convictions

10	Class A
9	Class B1
6	Class B2, C, or D
4	Class E, F, or G
2	Class H or I
1	Qualifying misdemeanors (Class A1 and 1 non-traffic misdemeanors; DWI, commercial DWI, and misdemeanor death by vehicle)
1	If all elements of the present offense are included in a prior offense, whether or not the prior offense was used in determining the defendant's prior record level. A judicial finding is required; a defendant cannot validly stipulate to this point. G.S. 15A-1340.14(b)(6).
1	If the defendant is on supervised or unsupervised probation, parole, or post-release supervision, serving a sentence, or on escape at the time of the offense. The State must provide 30 days' written notice if it intends to seek this point (use form AOC-CR-614) and then must prove it like an aggravating factor if it is not admitted to. G.S. 15A-1340.14(b)(7); -1340.16(a5).

Prior Record Levels

Level	Offenses Committed On/After 12/1/2009	Offenses Committed Before 12/1/2009
I	0–1 points	0 points
II	2–5	1–4
III	6–9	5–8
IV	10–13	9–14
V	14–17	15–18
VI	18+	19+

Prior Convictions That Count

- Only the most serious prior conviction from one calendar week of a single superior court. G.S. 15A-1340.14(d).
- Only one conviction from a single session of district court. G.S. 15A-1340.14(d).
- A prayer for judgment continued (PJC). State v. Canellas, 164 N.C. App. 775 (2004).
- A conviction resulting in G.S. 90-96 probation, if it has not yet been dismissed. State v. Hasty, 133 N.C. App. 563 (1999).
- Convictions in superior court, regardless of a pending appeal to the appellate division. G.S. 15A-1340.11(7).
- Qualifying convictions, regardless of when they arose (there is no statute of limitations). State v. Rich, 130 N.C. App. 113 (1998).
- Crimes from other jurisdictions, as described below.
- *For possession of firearm by felon*: The prior felony used to establish the person's status as a felon. State v. Best, 214 N.C. App. 39 (2011).
- *For failure to register as a sex offender:* The sex crime that caused the offender to register. State v. Harrison, 165 N.C. App. 332 (2004).

Prior Convictions That Do Not Count

- Class 2 and 3 misdemeanors.
- Misdemeanor traffic offenses other than DWI, commercial DWI, and misdemeanor death by vehicle.
- Infractions.
- Contempt. State v. Reaves, 142 N.C. App. 629 (2001).
- Juvenile adjudications.
- District court convictions on appeal or for which the time for appeal to superior court has not yet expired. G.S. 15A-1340.11(7).
- *For habitual felon:* Prior convictions used to establish habitual felon status. G.S. 14-7.6. When a defendant has multiple prior felony convictions from a single calendar week, one may be used to establish habitual felon status and another may be used for prior record points. State v. Truesdale, 123 N.C. App. 639 (1996).
- *For habitual breaking and entering:* Prior convictions used to establish habitual breaking and entering status. G.S. 14-7.31.
- *For habitual DWI:* Prior misdemeanor DWI convictions used to support a habitual DWI charge. State v. Gentry, 135 N.C. App. 107 (1999).

Notes

Proof. The State must prove a defendant's record by a preponderance of the evidence. Prior convictions are proved by stipulation, court or administrative records, or any other method found by the court to be reliable. For felony sentencing, the State must make all feasible efforts to obtain and present the defendant's full record. G.S. 15A-1340.14(f).

Out-of-state prior convictions. By default, an out-of-state felony is treated as a Class I felony (2 points), and an out-of-state misdemeanor is treated as a Class 3 misdemeanor (0 points). If the State or defendant proves by a preponderance of the evidence that the out-of-state offense is *substantially similar* to a North Carolina crime, the prior out-of-state conviction may count for points like the similar North Carolina crime. A defendant may stipulate that a crime is a felony or misdemeanor in another state, but not to its substantial similarity, which is a question of law that must be determined by the judge. The judge must compare the elements of the out-of-state crime to the elements of the purportedly similar North Carolina crime. State v. Hanton, 175 N.C. App. 250 (2006).

Date of determination. Prior record level is determined on the date a criminal judgment is entered, G.S. 15A-1340.11(7), and may include convictions for offenses that occurred after the offense now being sentenced, State v. Threadgill, 227 N.C. App. 175 (2013).

Prior offense classifications. If the offense class of a prior conviction has changed over time, use the classification assigned to the prior conviction as of the offense date of the crime now being sentenced. G.S. 15A-1340.14(c).

Habitualized prior felonies. Prior offenses that were sentenced under the habitual felon law count for points according to their original offense class, not the elevated habitual felon offense class. State v. Vaughn, 130 N.C. App. 456 (1998).

Ethical considerations. The State and the defendant may not agree to intentionally underreport a defendant's record to the court. Council of the N.C. State Bar, 2003 Formal Ethics Op. 5. A defendant may not misrepresent his or her record but may remain silent on the issue, even during the presentation of an inaccurate record, provided he or she was not the source of the inaccuracy. 1998 Formal Ethics Op. 5.

Suppression. The defendant may move to suppress a prior conviction obtained in violation of the right to counsel. G.S. 15A-980.

4 Consider Aggravating and Mitigating Factors

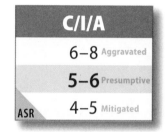

With findings of aggravating or mitigating factors, the court may depart from the presumptive range of sentence durations.

See **APPENDIX C** , Aggravating Factors, *and* **APPENDIX D** , Mitigating Factors.

Notes

Notice. The State must provide written notice of its intent to prove specific aggravating factors at least 30 days before trial or plea, unless the defendant waives the right to notice. G.S. 15A-1340.16(a6). (Use form AOC-CR-614.)

Pleading. Statutory aggravating factors need not be pled. Non-statutory (ad hoc) factors must be pled by indictment or other instrument. G.S. 15A-1340.16(a4).

Proof. Aggravating factors (except for factor 18a and possibly factor 12a) must be proved to the jury beyond a reasonable doubt, unless admitted to. G.S. 15A-1340.16(a). Admitted aggravating factors must be pled guilty to under G.S. 15A-1022.1; a mere stipulation is insufficient. The defendant bears the burden of proving mitigating factors to the judge by a preponderance of the evidence.

Jury procedure. The jury impaneled for trial may in the same trial determine aggravating factors, unless the court determines that the interests of justice require a separate proceeding. A defendant may admit to aggravating factors but plead not guilty to the underlying felony. Conversely, a defendant may plead guilty to a felony but contest aggravating factors. G.S. 15A-1340.16. If aggravating factors are not addressed at the charge conference held before the guilt-innocence phase of the trial, the trial court must hold a separate charge conference before instructing the jury during the sentencing phase. G.S. 15A-1231; State v. Hill, 235 N.C. App. 166 (2014).

Prohibited aggravating factors. Evidence necessary to prove an element of the offense may not be used to prove an aggravating factor. The same item of evidence may not be used to prove more than one aggravating factor. The defendant's exercise of the right to a jury trial is not an aggravating factor. G.S. 15A-1340.16.

Findings. Written findings of aggravating and mitigating factors are required only when the court departs from the presumptive range. G.S. 15A-1430.16(c). (Use form AOC-CR-605.)

Uncontroverted mitigating factors. If the court gives a sentence from the aggravated range, it must also make written findings of any presented mitigating factor supported by uncontroverted and manifestly credible evidence. State v. Wilkes, 225 N.C. App. 233 (2013).

Opportunity to prove. The court must allow the defendant an opportunity to present evidence of mitigating factors. State v. Knott, 164 N.C. App. 212 (2004).

Weighing of factors. Weighing aggravating and mitigating factors is a matter of judicial discretion and not a mathematical balance. State v. Vaughters, 219 N.C. App.

Figure 1. Minimum, and Corresponding Maximum, Sentence Relationship

356 (2012) (no error to find that one aggravating factor outweighed nineteen mitigating factors).

Judge's discretion. The trial court must consider evidence of aggravating and mitigating factors offered by the parties, State v. Kemp, 153 N.C. App. 231 (2002), but the decision to depart from the presumptive range is entirely within the court's discretion. The court may enter a presumptive sentence even after finding that mitigating factors outweigh aggravating factors. State v. Bivens, 155 N.C. App. 645 (2002).

5 Select a Sentence of Imprisonment

The court imposes a sentence of imprisonment as part of every sentence, including probationary sentences. The court then determines (in step 6) whether the defendant will be incarcerated for that term (Active punishment) or whether the sentence will be suspended and served only upon revocation of probation (Intermediate or Community punishment). The only exception to the requirement for the court to select a sentence of imprisonment is a sentence to a fine only, which is permissible as a Community punishment. G.S. 15A-1340.17(b).

Minimum Sentence (G.S. 15A-1340.17(c))

The court selects a minimum sentence from the desired range (presumptive, aggravated, or mitigated) of the appropriate cell of the sentencing grid. The range of permissible minimum sentences is set out on the left-hand page of each sentencing grid.

Maximum Sentence (G.S. 15A-1340.17(d)–(f))

The maximum sentence corresponding to the selected minimum sentence is displayed in the table on the right-hand page of each sentencing grid. Use the portion of the table applicable to the offense class being sentenced (Class F–I at the bottom; Class B1–E at the top, as shown in figure 1), use the maximum in parentheses for Class B1–E felonies that require sex offender registration.

Life Sentences

In general, life sentences under Structured Sentencing are sentences to life imprisonment without parole—sometimes referred to as "natural life" sentences. For defendants convicted of first-degree murder who are under age 18 at the time of the offense, the court must follow the procedure set out in G.S. 15A-1340.19B, enacted in response to *Miller v. Alabama*, 567 U.S. 460 (2012). If the sole basis for the conviction was the felony murder rule, the court must impose a sentence of life imprisonment with the possibility of parole. If the conviction was not the result of the felony murder rule, the court must conduct a hearing to consider mitigating circumstances related to the defendant's youth and whether the defendant should be sentenced to life with or without the possibility of parole. Defendants sentenced to life with the possibility of parole are eligible for parole after 25 years of imprisonment.

C/I/A
6–8
5–6
ASR 4–5

6 Choose a Sentence Disposition

The court must choose a disposition for each sentence. There are three possible sentence dispositions under Structured Sentencing: Active, Intermediate, and Community. The letters shown in each grid cell (A, I, and/or C) indicate which dispositions are permissible in that cell.

Active Punishment (G.S. 15A-1340.11(1))

An Active punishment requires that the defendant serve the imposed sentence of imprisonment in prison, in the custody of the Division of Adult Correction and Juvenile Justice (DACJJ).

Intermediate Punishment (G.S. 15A-1340.11(6))

Intermediate punishment requires that the court suspend the sentence of imprisonment and impose SUPERVISED probation. Intermediate probation may include drug treatment court, special probation (a split sentence), or any of the "community and intermediate probation conditions" in G.S. 15A-1343(a1). *See* "Probationary Sentences," page 26.

Community Punishment (G.S. 15A-1340.11(2))

Community punishment requires that the court suspend the sentence of imprisonment and impose SUPERVISED or UNSUPERVISED probation. Community probation may not include drug treatment court or special probation, but it may include any of the "community and intermediate probation conditions" in G.S. 15A-1343(a1). A Community punishment also may consist of a fine only. *See* "Probationary Sentences," page 26.

Post-Release Supervision (PRS) (G.S. 15A-1368.2)		Release to Post-Release Supervision (months before maximum)	Post-Release Supervision Period
Class F–I felonies committed on/after 12/1/2011	Nonreportable crimes	9 months	9 months
	Reportable sex crimes	9 months	5 years
Class B1–E felonies committed on/after 12/1/2011	Nonreportable crimes	12 months	12 months
	Reportable sex crimes	60 months	5 years
Class F–I felonies committed before 12/1/2011	All crimes	N/A (no PRS)	N/A (no PRS)
Class B1–E felonies committed before 12/1/2011	Nonreportable crimes	9 months	9 months
	Reportable sex crimes	9 months	5 years

All felonies committed on or after December 1, 2011, that result in imprisonment—pursuant either to an Active sentence or a suspended sentence activated upon revocation of probation—require post-release supervision (PRS). Defendants subject to PRS are automatically released from prison a certain number of months (indicated in the table) before attaining their maximum sentence. The remaining term of imprisonment operates as a suspended sentence during a period of PRS, the length of which varies depending on the offense date, offense class, and whether or not the crime requires registration as a sex offender, as shown in the table. The remaining imprisonment is subject to activation upon certain findings of violation by the Post-Release Supervision and Parole Commission. G.S. 15A-1368.3.

Purposes of Sentencing

Under G.S. 15A-1340.12, the primary purposes of sentencing in North Carolina are to:

Punish the defendant, commensurate with the injury the offense has caused, taking into account factors that may diminish or increase the defendant's culpability.

Protect the public by restraining the defendant.

Rehabilitate the defendant.

Restore the defendant to the community as a lawful citizen.

Deter criminal behavior by others.

7 Review Additional Issues, as Appropriate

The section of this handbook on "Additional Issues" includes information on the following matters that may arise at sentencing:
- Fines, costs, and other fees
- Restitution
- Sex crimes
- Sentencing multiple convictions
- Jail credit
- Sentence reduction credits
- DNA sample
- Diversions (deferred prosecution, conditional discharge, and prayer for judgment continued (PJC))
- Work release
- Obtaining additional information for sentencing

Felony Enhancement and Mitigation Options

Felony Enhancements

Habitual Felon

Eligibility. The defendant has three qualifying prior felonies (each committed after conviction for the one before it, counting no more than one committed before age 18) and is now convicted of a felony. G.S. 14-7.1.

Sentencing. Four-class enhancement, but no higher than Class C (unless the present felony is a Class A, B1, or B2 offense, in which case the defendant is sentenced according to the regular classification). G.S. 14-7.6. The enhanced sentence must run consecutively to any sentence being served, *id.*, but may be consolidated or run concurrently with other sentences imposed at the same time, State v. Haymond, 203 N.C. App. 151 (2010).

Habitual Breaking and Entering

Eligibility. The defendant has one prior "felony offense of breaking and entering" (first- or second-degree burglary, felony breaking or entering, breaking out of a dwelling house burglary, breaking or entering a building that is a place of worship, or any repealed or superseded offense or offense from another jurisdiction that is substantially equivalent to those offenses) and is now convicted of another felony offense of breaking and entering. G.S. 14-7.26.

Sentencing. Sentenced as a Class E felon. The enhanced sentence must run consecutively to any sentence being served by the defendant. G.S. 14-7.31.

Violent Habitual Felon

Eligibility. The defendant has two prior violent felony convictions (any Class A through Class E felony or substantially similar offense from another jurisdiction), with the second committed after conviction for the first, and is now convicted of another violent felony. G.S. 14-7.7.

Sentencing. Life without parole. The enhanced sentence must run consecutively to any sentence being served by the defendant. G.S. 14-7.12.

Armed Habitual Felon

Eligibility. The defendant has one or more prior "firearm-related felony" (any felony in which the person used or displayed a firearm while committing the felony) and is now convicted of another firearm-related felony. G.S. 14-7.36.

Sentencing. Sentenced as a Class C felon (unless the present felony is a Class A, B1, or B2 offense), with a mandatory minimum sentence of 120 months. The enhanced sentence must run consecutively to any sentence being served by the defendant. G.S. 14-7.41.

Protective Order Violation

Eligibility. The defendant committed a felony at a time when he or she knew the behavior was prohibited by a valid protective order.

Sentencing. One-class enhancement. G.S. 50B-4.1(d).

Bullet-Proof Vest Enhancement

Eligibility. The defendant wore or had in his or her immediate possession a bullet-proof vest at the time of a felony. The enhancement does not apply when the evidence of the bullet-proof vest is needed to prove an element of the felony.

Sentencing. One-class enhancement. G.S. 15A-1340.16C.

Firearm/Deadly Weapon Enhancement

Eligibility. The defendant actually possessed and used, displayed, or threatened the use or display of a firearm or deadly weapon in committing a felony. The enhancement does not apply to defendants sentenced to probation, or when the enhancing facts are needed to prove an element of the felony. Enhancing facts must be charged by indictment or information.

Sentencing. Minimum sentence increased as follows:

- Class B1 through E felonies: 72-month enhancement
- Class F and G felonies: 36-month enhancement
- Class H and I felonies: 12-month enhancement

Use the maximum sentence that corresponds to the enhanced minimum. G.S. 15A-1340.16A.

Second/Subsequent Class B1 Felony

Eligibility. The defendant has one or more prior Class B1 felony convictions and is now convicted of a Class B1 felony committed against a victim age 13 or younger. The defendant must be charged by indictment or information as provided in G.S. 15A-1340.16B(d). The enhancement does not apply if mitigating factors are present.

Sentencing. Life without parole. G.S. 15A-1340.16B.

Criminal Gang Activity Enhancement

Eligibility. The defendant is convicted of a Class C through I felony that is found to have been committed by "criminal gang members" as part of "criminal gang activity," as those terms are defined in G.S. 14-50.16A. Applies only to offenses committed on or after December 1, 2017.

Sentencing. One-class enhancement, capped at Class C. The enhanced sentence must run consecutively to any sentence being served by the defendant. G.S. 15A-1340.16E(a).

Criminal Gang Leader or Organizer Enhancement

Eligibility. The defendant is convicted of a Class C through I felony that is found to have been committed by "criminal gang members" as part of "criminal gang activity," as those terms are defined in G.S. 14-50.16A, *and* the defendant is a "criminal gang leader or organizer," as that term is defined in G.S. 14-50.16A(3). Applies only to offenses committed on or after December 1, 2017.

Sentencing. Two-class enhancement, capped at Class C. The enhanced sentence must run consecutively to any sentence being served by the defendant. G.S. 15A-1340.16E(b).

Felony Mitigation

Grid cells in which EM might be possible are flagged with this symbol.

Extraordinary Mitigation (EM)

Eligibility. A defendant with 4 or fewer prior record points is convicted of a Class B2, C, or D felony, and the court finds that:

1. Extraordinary mitigating factors of a kind significantly greater than in a normal case are present,
2. Those factors substantially outweigh any factors in aggravation, and
3. It would be a manifest injustice to impose an Active punishment in the case.

Extraordinary mitigation does not apply in drug trafficking or drug trafficking conspiracy cases.

Sentencing. The defendant may be sentenced to Intermediate probation. Use form AOC-CR-606. G.S. 15A-1340.13(g)–(h).

Advanced Supervised Release (ASR)

Grid cells in which ASR might be possible are flagged with this symbol.

Eligibility. The court may impose an ASR date for a defendant who receives an Active sentence for a felony in the following grid cells:

- Class D, Prior Record Levels I–III
- Class E, Prior Record Levels I–IV
- Class F, Prior Record Levels I–V
- All Class G and H felonies

ASR does not apply if the prosecutor objects.

Sentencing. In addition to the regular sentence, the sentencing judge orders the defendant into the prison system's ASR program and includes an ASR date in the judgment. The ASR date flows from the regular sentence as follows:

- For any regular sentence from the presumptive or aggravated range: The ASR date is the lowest permissible minimum sentence from the mitigated range in the defendant's grid cell.
- For any regular sentence from the mitigated range: The ASR date is 80 percent of the imposed minimum sentence.

ASR inmates who complete "risk reduction incentives" (or who are unable to do so through no fault of their own) are released onto post-release supervision on their ASR date. Inmates who do not complete the ASR program are released according to their regular sentence. G.S. 15A-1340.18.

Substantial Assistance

Drug trafficking only. *See* "Drug Trafficking Sentencing," page 49.

Misdemeanor Sentencing

1 Determine the Offense Class

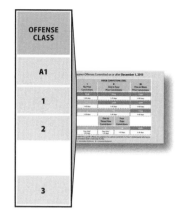

North Carolina misdemeanors are assigned to one of four offense classes—Class A1, 1, 2, and 3, from most to least serious. Identify the offense class of the crime being sentenced. *See* **APPENDIX B**, Offense Class Table for Misdemeanors.

Offense Class Reductions

Unless otherwise provided by law, the following step-down rules apply for attempts, conspiracies, and solicitations to commit a misdemeanor:
- Attempt—one class lower (G.S. 14-2.5)
- Conspiracy—one class lower (G.S. 14-2.4)
- Solicitation—Always a Class 3 misdemeanor (G.S. 14-2.6)

Offense Class Enhancements

With appropriate factual findings, the offense class of certain misdemeanors may be increased under the enhancements set out below. Additional procedural requirements apply.

Criminal Gang Activity (G.S. 14-50.22)
- One offense class higher (Class A1 misdemeanor enhanced to Class I felony)

Committed Because of the Victim's Race, Color, Religion, Nationality, or Country of Origin (G.S. 14-3(c))
- Class 2 and 3 misdemeanors enhanced to Class 1 misdemeanor
- Class 1 and A1 misdemeanors enhanced to Class H felony

2 Determine the Prior Conviction Level

The defendant is assigned to one of three prior conviction levels (I through III) based on his or her criminal history.

Level	Prior Convictions
I	No prior convictions
II	1–4 prior convictions
III	5 or more prior convictions

Prior Convictions That Count
- Only one prior conviction from a single session of district court, or in a single week of superior court or court in another jurisdiction. G.S. 15A-1340.21(d).
- District court convictions, when the defendent has not given notice of appeal and the time for appeal has expired. G.S. 15A-1340.11(7).
- Convictions in superior court, regardless of a pending appeal to the appellate division. G.S. 15A-1340.11(7).
- Convictions from another state, the Armed Forces, the federal courts, or another country. G.S. 15A-1340.11(7).
- Qualifying convictions, regardless of when they arose (there is no statute of limitations). State v. Rich, 130 N.C. App. 113 (1998).
- A prayer for judgment continued (PJC). State v. Canellas, 164 N.C. App. 775 (2004).
- A conviction resulting in G.S. 90-96 probation, if it has not yet been dismissed. State v. Hasty, 133 N.C. App. 563 (1999).

Prior Convictions That Do Not Count

- Infractions.
- Contempt. State v. Reaves, 142 N.C. App. 629 (2001).
- Juvenile adjudications.
- District court convictions on appeal, or for which the time for appeal to superior court has not yet expired. G.S. 15A-1340.11(7).

Notes

Proof. The State must prove a defendant's record by a preponderance of the evidence. Prior convictions are proved by stipulation, court or administrative records, or any other method found by the court to be reliable. G.S. 15A-1340.21(c).

Date of determination. Prior record level is determined on the date a criminal judgment is entered, G.S. 15A-1340.11(7), and may include convictions for offenses that occurred after the offense now being sentenced, State v. Threadgill, 227 N.C. App. 175 (2013).

Ethical considerations. The State and defendant may not agree to intentionally underreport a defendant's record to the court. Council of the N.C. State Bar, 2003 Formal Ethics Op. 5. A defendant may not misrepresent his or her record but may remain silent on the issue, even during the presentation of an inaccurate record, provided he or she was not the source of the inaccuracy. 1998 Formal Ethics Op. 5.

Suppression. The defendant may move to suppress a prior conviction obtained in violation of his or her right to counsel. G.S. 15A-980.

3 Select a Sentence of Imprisonment

The court imposes a sentence of imprisonment as part of every sentence, including probationary sentences. The court then determines (in step 4) whether the defendant will be incarcerated for that term (Active punishment) or whether the sentence will be suspended and served only upon revocation of probation (Intermediate or Community punishment).

C/I/A
1–60 days

Term of Imprisonment

For misdemeanor sentencing, the court selects a single term of imprisonment from the range shown in the applicable grid cell; unlike felony sentencing, there is no minimum and maximum.

For sentences imposed on or after October 1, 2014, misdemeanor sentences of 90 days or less are served in the local jail, except as provided in G.S. 148-32.1. Misdemeanor sentences in excess of 90 days are served in the Statewide Misdemeanant Confinement Program, through which the N.C. Sheriffs' Association will find space for the inmate in a jail that has volunteered beds to the program. *See* APPENDIX G , Place of Confinement Chart, for additional rules.

Fine-Only Sentences

The only exception to the requirement for the court to select a sentence of imprisonment is a sentence to a fine only, which is permissible as a Community punishment. For Class 3 misdemeanors committed on or after December 1, 2013, unless otherwise provided for a specific offense, the judgment for a defendant with no more than three prior convictions shall consist of a fine only. G.S. 15A-1340.23(d). Use form AOC-CR-629.

Limit on Consecutive Sentences

The cumulative term of imprisonment for consecutive misdemeanor sentences may not exceed twice the maximum sentence authorized for the class and prior conviction level of the most serious offense. If all convictions are for Class 3 misdemeanors, consecutive sentences shall not be imposed. G.S. 15A-1340.22(a).

4 Choose a Sentence Disposition

The court must choose a disposition for each sentence. There are three possible sentence dispositions under Structured Sentencing: Active, Intermediate, and Community. The letters shown in each grid cell (A, I, and/or C) indicate which dispositions are permissible in that cell.

Active Punishment (G.S. 15A-1340.11(1))

An Active punishment requires that the defendant serve the imposed sentence of imprisonment in jail or prison.

Intermediate Punishment (G.S. 15A-1340.11(6))

Intermediate punishment requires that the court suspend the sentence of imprisonment and impose SUPERVISED probation. Intermediate probation may include drug treatment court, special probation (a split sentence), or any of the "community and intermediate probation conditions" in G.S. 15A-1343(a1). *See* "Probationary Sentences," page 26.

Community Punishment (G.S. 15A-1340.11(2))

Community punishment requires that the court suspend the sentence of imprisonment and impose SUPERVISED or UNSUPERVISED probation. Community probation may not include drug treatment court or special probation, but it may include any of the "community and intermediate probation conditions" in G.S. 15A-1343(a1). A Community punishment also may consist of a fine only. *See* "Probationary Sentences," page 26.

5 Review Additional Issues, as Appropriate

The "Additional Issues" section of this handbook includes information on the following matters that may arise at sentencing:

- Fines, costs, and other fees
- Restitution
- Sex Crimes
- Sentencing multiple convictions
- Jail credit
- Sentence reduction credits
- DNA sample
- Diversions (deferred prosecution, conditional discharge, and prayer for judgment continued (PJC))
- Work release
- Obtaining additional information for sentencing

C/I/A
1–60 days

Active Punishment Exception

An Active sentence to time already served is permissible for any misdemeanant with pretrial jail credit, even if an Active punishment is not ordinarily allowed in his or her grid cell. G.S. 15A-1340.20(c1).

Purposes of Sentencing

Under G.S. 15A-1340.12, the primary purposes of sentencing in North Carolina are to:

Punish the defendant, commensurate with the injury the offense has caused, taking into account factors that may diminish or increase the defendant's culpability.

Protect the public by restraining the defendant.

Rehabilitate the defendant.

Restore the defendant to the community as a lawful citizen.

Deter criminal behavior by others.

DWI Sentencing

The following offenses are sentenced pursuant to G.S. 20-179 rather than Structured Sentencing:

- G.S. 20-138.1 (impaired driving).
- G.S. 20-138.2 (impaired driving in a commercial vehicle).
- Second or subsequent conviction of
  - G.S. 20-138.2A (operating a commercial vehicle after consuming alcohol) or
  - G.S. 20-138.2B (operating a school bus, child care vehicle, emergency, or law enforcement vehicle after consuming).
- A person convicted of impaired driving under G.S. 20-138.1 under the common law concept of aiding and abetting is subject to Level Five punishment. The judge need not make any findings of grossly aggravating, aggravating, or mitigating factors in such cases.

1 Determine the Applicable Law

Choose the appropriate sentencing grid and potentially applicable sentencing factors (form AOC-CR-311) based upon the date of the defendant's offense.

> **Offenses committed on or after October 1, 2013**

> **Offenses committed on or after December 1, 2012, and before October 1, 2013**

> **Offenses committed on or after December 1, 2011, and before December 1, 2012**

> **Offenses committed on or after December 1, 2007, and before December 1, 2011**

2 Determine Whether Any Grossly Aggravating Factors Exist

There are four grossly aggravating factors:

(1) a qualifying prior conviction for an offense involving impaired driving;
(2) driving while license revoked for an impaired driving revocation;
(3) serious injury to another person caused by the defendant's impaired driving; and
(4) driving with one of the following types of individuals in the vehicle:
  (i)   a child under the age of 18,
  (ii) a person with the mental development of a child under 18, or
  (iii) a person with a physical disability preventing unaided exit from the vehicle.

In superior court, the jury is the finder of fact for all aggravating (including grossly aggravating) factors other than whether a prior conviction exists under G.S. 20-179(c)(1) or (d)(5). Any factor admitted by the defendant is treated as though it was found by the jury. In district court, the judge is the finder of fact.

3 Enter Factors on Determination of Sentencing Factors Form (AOC-CR-311)

If the jury finds aggravating factors, the court must enter those factors on the Determination of Sentencing Factors form. Judge-found grossly aggravating factors must also be entered on the form.

4 Count the Grossly Aggravating Factors

If there are no grossly aggravating factors, skip to step 6.

5 Determine the Sentencing Level

If there are three or more grossly aggravating factors, the judge must impose Aggravated Level One punishment. (For offenses committed before December 1, 2011, Level One punishment must be imposed in any case in which two or more grossly aggravating factors are found.)

If the grossly aggravating factor in G.S. 20-179(c)(4) exists (driving while a child, person with the mental capacity of a child, or a disabled person is in the vehicle) or if two other grossly aggravating factors exist, the judge must impose Level One punishment. (For offenses committed before December 1, 2011, the presence of factor G.S. 20-179(c)(4) does not require Level One punishment.)

If only one grossly aggravating factor exists (other than the factor in G.S. 20-179(c)(4)), the judge must impose Level Two punishment.

6 Consider Aggravating and Mitigating Factors

If one or more grossly aggravating factors is found, decide whether to consider aggravating and mitigating factors in determining the appropriate sentence within the applicable level of punishment.

In district court, the judge may elect not to formally determine the presence of aggravating or mitigating factors if there are grossly aggravating factors. In superior court, the jury will determine before the sentencing hearing whether there are aggravating factors. If one or more grossly aggravating factors is found, a superior court judge may elect not to formally determine the presence of mitigating factors. If the judge elects *not* to determine such factors, skip to step 10.

7 Determine Aggravating Factors

If there are no grossly aggravating factors, or if the judge elects to consider aggravating and mitigating factors in a case in which there are grossly aggravating factors, determine whether aggravating factors exist. The State bears the burden of proving beyond a reasonable doubt that any aggravating factor exists.

There are nine aggravating factors, eight of them defined and a ninth "catch-all" aggravating factor:

1. Gross impairment of the defendant's faculties while driving or an alcohol concentration of 0.15 or more.
2. Especially reckless or dangerous driving.
3. Negligent driving that led to a reportable accident.
4. Driving by the defendant while his or her driver's license was revoked.
5. Two or more prior convictions of certain motor vehicle offenses within five years of the instant offense or one or more prior convictions of an offense involving impaired driving that occurred more than seven years before the instant offense.
6. Conviction under G.S. 20-141.5 of speeding to elude.
7. Conviction under G.S. 20-141 of speeding by the defendant by at least 30 miles per hour over the legal limit.
8. Passing a stopped school bus in violation of G.S. 20-217.
9. Any other factor that aggravates the seriousness of the offense.

Except for the fifth factor (which involves prior convictions), the conduct constituting the aggravating factor must occur during the same transaction or occurrence as the impaired driving offense.

Note any aggravating factors found on the Determination of Sentencing Factors form.

8 Determine Mitigating Factors

Determine whether mitigating factors exist.

Mitigating factors are set forth in subsections (e)(1)–(7) of G.S. 20-179. There are eight mitigating factors (one is set forth in G.S. 20-179(e)(6a)), including a catch-all factor. The judge in both district and superior courts determines the existence of any mitigating factor. The defendant bears the burden of proving by a preponderance of the evidence that a mitigating factor exists. Except for the factors in subdivisions (4), (6), (6a), and (7), the conduct constituting the mitigating factor must occur during the same transaction or occurrence as the covered offense.

The following are mitigating factors listed by the subdivision of G.S. 20-179(e) in which they appear.

(1) Slight impairment of the defendant's faculties, resulting solely from alcohol, and an alcohol concentration that did not exceed 0.09 at any relevant time after the driving.

(2) Slight impairment of the defendant's faculties, resulting solely from alcohol, with no chemical analysis having been available to the defendant.

(3) Driving that was safe and lawful except for the defendant's impairment.

(4) A safe driving record.

(5) Impairment caused primarily by a lawfully prescribed drug for an existing medical condition, and the amount of drug taken was within the prescribed dosage.

(6) Voluntary submission to a substance abuse assessment and to treatment.

(6a) Completion of a substance abuse assessment, compliance with its recommendations, and 60 days of continuous abstinence from alcohol consumption, as proven by a continuous alcohol monitoring (CAM) system.

(7) Any other factor that mitigates the seriousness of the offense.

Record any factors found on the Determination of Sentencing Factors form.

Note: The fact that the driver was suffering from alcoholism, drug addiction, diminished capacity, or mental disease or defect is ***not*** a mitigating factor. Evidence of these matters may be received in the sentencing hearing, however, for use by the judge in formulating terms and conditions of sentence after determining the punishment level.

9 Weigh Aggravating and Mitigating Factors

If aggravating factors substantially outweigh any mitigating factors, or if there are only aggravating factors, find that the defendant is subject to Level Three punishment.

If there are no aggravating or mitigating factors, or if aggravating factors are counterbalanced by mitigating factors, find that the defendant is subject to Level Four punishment.

If the mitigating factors substantially outweigh any aggravating factors, or if there are only mitigating factors, find that the defendant is subject to Level Five punishment.

10 Select a Sentence of Imprisonment

The imprisonment, mandatory probation conditions, and fines for each level of impaired driving sentenced under G.S. 20-179 are set forth in the DWI sentencing grids. The judgment must impose a maximum term and may impose a minimum term. A judgment may state that a term is both the minimum and maximum term. G.S. 15A-1351(b).

Place of Confinement

For sentences imposed on or after January 1, 2015, imprisonment of any duration under G.S. 20-179, other than imprisonment required as a condition of special probation, is served in the Statewide Misdemeanant Confinement Program. All imprisonment imposed as a condition of special probation must be served in a designated local confinement or treatment facility—regardless of whether the imprisonment is for continuous or noncontinuous periods. *See* **APPENDIX G**, Place of Confinement Chart, for additional rules.

11 Review Additional Issues, as Appropriate

The section of this handbook on "Additional Issues" includes information on the following matters that may arise at sentencing:

- Fines, costs, and other fees
- Restitution
- Sentencing multiple convictions
- Jail credit
- Sentence reduction credits
- DWI parole
- Obtaining additional information for sentencing

Additional Issues

Monetary Obligations

Fines

Any sentence may include a fine. G.S. 15A-1361; -1340.17; -1340.23. Unless otherwise provided for a specific crime, the amount of the fine is in the discretion of the court. Unless otherwise provided by law, the maximum fine for a Class 3 misdemeanor is $200, and the maximum fine for a Class 2 misdemeanor is $1,000. G.S. 15A-1340.23(b). The fine for a local ordinance violation may not exceed $50 unless the ordinance expressly provides for a larger fine, which in no case may exceed $500. G.S. 14-4.

For Class 3 misdemeanors committed on or after December 1, 2013, unless otherwise provided for a specific offense, the judgment for a defendant with no more than three prior convictions shall consist of a fine only. G.S. 15A-1340.23(b). Use form AOC-CR-629.

Unpaid fines may, upon a determination of default, be responded to as provided in G.S. 15A-1364 and docketed as a civil judgment as provided in G.S. 15A-1365.

Costs

Court costs apply by default in every case in which the defendant is convicted, regardless of sentence disposition. Only upon entry of a written order, supported by findings of fact and conclusions of law, determining that there is just cause may the court waive costs. G.S. 7A-304(a). No cost may be waived or remitted without providing notice (at least 15 days by first-class mail) and an opportunity to be heard to all government entities directly affected. G.S. 7A-304(a). The Administrative Office of the Courts provides a statewide monthly notice to all potentially affected entities that might satisfy this requirement. Unpaid costs may, upon a determination of default, be responded to as provided in G.S. 15A-1364 and docketed as a civil judgment as provided in G.S. 15A-1365.

Attorney Fees

Attorney fees are ordered and docketed as provided in G.S. 7A-455, under rules adopted by the Office of Indigent Defense Services. An additional $60 attorney appointment fee applies under G.S. 7A-455.1. A defendant is entitled to notice and a hearing informing him or her of the appointed attorney's total hours or the total fee before the court may impose a judgment for attorney fees. State v. Jacobs, 172 N.C. App. 220 (2005).

Probation Supervision Fees

Supervised probationers pay a supervision fee of $40 per month. The court may exempt the defendant from paying the fee for good cause and upon motion of the probationer. G.S. 15A-1343(c1).

Probationary Jail Fees

Probationers may, in the discretion of the court, be ordered to pay a $40 fee for each day of jail confinement imposed as a condition of probation. This fee is not to be confused with the $10 per day fee for **pretrial** confinement, which is a court cost and applicable by default unless waived for just cause. G.S. 7A-313.

Electronic House Arrest (EHA) Fee

Probationers sentenced to electronic house arrest (EHA) pay a one-time fee of $90, plus an additional fee reflecting the actual daily cost ($4.48 per day as of June 2018). The court may exempt the defendant from paying the fee for good cause and upon motion of the probationer. G.S. 15A-1343(c2).

Community Service Fee
Defendants ordered to complete community service pay a fee of $250 per sentencing transaction. G.S. 143B-708.

Restitution
The court must consider ordering restitution from a criminal defendant to a victim in every case. G.S. 15A-1340.34(a). The court shall order restitution to the victim of any offense covered under the Crime Victims' Rights Act (CVRA). G.S. 15A-1340.34(b). *See* **APPENDIX E**, Crimes Covered under the Crime Victims' Rights Act.

Restitution *May* Be Ordered for the Following:

- **In bodily injury cases:** the costs of medical care, therapy, rehabilitation, and lost income. If an offense results in a victim's death, the court may order restitution for funeral and related expenses. G.S. 15A-1340.35(a)(1).
- **In property cases:** if return of the property is impossible, impractical, or inadequate, the value of the property as of the date of offense or sentencing. G.S. 15A-1340.35(a)(2), (a)(4).
- To a person other than the victim, or to any organization, corporation, or association that provided assistance to the victim and is subrogated to the rights of the victim. G.S. 15A-1340.37(b).

Restitution *May Not* Be Ordered for the Following:

- A victim's pain and suffering. State v. Wilson, 158 N.C. App. 235 (2003).
- As punitive damages. State v. Burkhead, 85 N.C. App. 535 (1987).

Notes
Proof of the restitution amount. The restitution amount must be supported by evidence adduced at trial or at the sentencing hearing, or by stipulation. The standard of proof is a preponderance of the evidence. State v. Tate, 187 N.C. App. 593 (2007). A prosecutor's statement or restitution worksheet, standing alone, is insufficient to support an award of restitution.

Ability to pay. The court must consider the defendant's ability to pay restitution. The burden of demonstrating the defendant's inability to pay restitution is on the defendant. *Id.*; G.S. 15A-1340.36(a).

Active cases. The court must consider recommending that restitution be paid out of any work-release earnings or as a condition of post-release supervision. G.S. 15A-1340.36(c).

Civil judgments. In CVRA cases, restitution orders exceeding $250 may be enforced as a civil judgment as provided in G.S. 15A-1340.38(b). If initially ordered as a condition of probation, the judgment may be executed upon the defendant's property only when probation is terminated or revoked and the judge has made a finding that a sum certain remains owed. G.S. 15A-1340.38(c). (Use form AOC-CR-612.) There is no clear authority to order restitution as a civil judgment in non-CVRA cases.

Remission. No restitution order may be remitted without notice (at least 15 days by first-class mail) and opportunity to be heard to the district attorney, the victim, the victim's estate, and any other recipient of restitution. G.S. 15A-1340.39.

> **Victims of Unconvicted Conduct**
> Restitution must be limited to the victims of the crime of conviction. G.S. 15A-1340.34(a). There is no statutory authority to order restitution to victims of charges dismissed pursuant to a plea agreement. State v. Murphy, ___ N.C. App. ___, ___ S.E.2d ___ (Aug. 21, 2018).

Sex Crimes
See **APPENDIX F**, Crimes Requiring Sex Offender Registration.

Satellite-Based Monitoring Determination Hearing
When sentencing a crime that requires sex offender registration, the court must conduct the hearing required by G.S. 14-208.40A, at which it will make findings related to registration and determine whether the defendant is required to enroll in

satellite-based monitoring (SBM). (Use form AOC-CR-615.) At the hearing, the court must, in light of *Grady v. North Carolina*, 135 S. Ct. 1368 (2015), determine whether SBM is a reasonable search. The State has the burden of establishing reasonableness, which is based on the totality of the circumstances, including the nature and purpose of the search and the extent to which it intrudes upon reasonable privacy expectations. State v. Blue, 783 S.E.2d 524 (2016).

Notice of Duty to Register

When sentencing a sex offender to probation, the court must give the defendant notice of his or her duty to register. G.S. 14-208.8(b). (Use form AOC-CR-261.)

No-Contact Order

At sentencing, the district attorney may ask the court to enter a permanent no-contact order prohibiting the defendant from having any direct or indirect contact with the victim of the offense. A violation of a no-contact order is a Class A1 misdemeanor. G.S. 15A-1340.50; State v. Barnett, 369 N.C. 298 (2016). (Use form AOC-CR-620.)

Sentencing Multiple Convictions

Consolidation

If a defendant is convicted of more than one offense at the same time, the court may consolidate the convictions and impose a single judgment with a sentence appropriate for the most serious offense. G.S. 15A-1340.15(b) (felonies); -1340.22(b) (misdemeanors).

DWI Two or more impaired driving charges may not be consolidated for judgment. Such sentences may, however, run concurrently. An impaired driving conviction sentenced under G.S. 20-179 may be consolidated with a charge carrying greater punishment.

Concurrent Sentences

Unless otherwise specified by the judge, all sentences of imprisonment run concurrently with one another. G.S. 15A-1340.15(a); -1354(a).

Consecutive Sentences

Generally, the judge may order one sentence of imprisonment to run at the expiration of another sentence. Note the following:

Single-sentence rule. When felony sentences are run consecutively, the Division of Adult Correction and Juvenile Justice (DACJJ) treats them as a single sentence. The aggregate minimum sentence is the sum of all of the individual minimum sentences. The aggregate maximum sentence is the sum of all the individual maximum sentences, less 12 months for each second and subsequent Class B1–E felonies, less 60 months for each second or subsequent Class B1–E reportable sex crime, and less 9 months for each second and subsequent Class F–I felony. The defendant will serve a single term of supervised release upon his or her release from prison, the length of which is dictated by the longest post-release supervision term to which the defendant is subject. G.S. 15A-1354(b).

Mandatory consecutive sentences. Some laws require a sentence to run consecutively to any other sentence being served by the defendant: habitual felon (G.S. 14-7.6); violent habitual felon (G.S. 14-7.12); armed habitual felon (G.S. 14-7.41); habitual breaking and entering (G.S. 14-7.31); habitual impaired driving (G.S. 20-138.5(b)); drug trafficking (G.S. 90-95(h)). These laws allow for concurrent or consolidated sentences for convictions sentenced at the same time. State v. Bozeman, 115 N.C. App. 658 (1994).

Limit on consecutive sentences for misdemeanors. The cumulative term of imprisonment for consecutive misdemeanor sentences may not exceed twice the maximum sentence authorized for the class and prior conviction level of the most serious offense.

If all convictions are for Class 3 misdemeanors, consecutive sentences shall not be imposed. G.S. 15A-1340.22(a).

Probationary Sentences

Suspended sentences may (consistent with the limitations described above) be set to run concurrently with or consecutively to one another in the event of revocation. Probation periods themselves, however, must run concurrently with one another. G.S. 15A-1346(a). The court may order a probation period to run consecutively to an Active sentence—an arrangement sometimes referred to as a contingent sentence. G.S. 15A-1346(b).

Jail Credit

A defendant must receive credit for the total amount of time he or she has spent in any State or local correctional, mental, or other institution as a result of the charge that culminated in the sentence or the incident from which the charge arose, including credit for all time spent in custody pending trial, trial de novo, appeal, retrial, or pending parole, probation, or post-release supervision revocation hearing. G.S. 15-196.1. The presiding judge must determine jail credit. G.S. 15-196.4.

Count for Jail Credit

- Pretrial confinement and time spent in confinement awaiting a probation violation hearing. G.S. 15-196.1.
- The active portion of a split sentence. State v. Farris, 336 N.C. 552 (1994).
- Time spent at DART Cherry as a condition of probation. State v. Lutz, 177 N.C. App. 140 (2006). Likely also applies to time spent at the Black Mountain Substance Abuse Treatment Center for Women.
- Presentence commitment for study. State v. Powell, 11 N.C. App. 194 (1971).
- Hospitalization to determine competency to stand trial. State v. Lewis, 18 N.C. App. 681 (1973).
- Time spent in confinement in another state awaiting extradition when the defendant was held in the other state solely based on North Carolina charges. Childers v. Laws, 558 F. Supp. 1284 (W.D.N.C. 1983).
- Time spent imprisoned for contempt under G.S. 15A-1344(e1). State v. Belcher, 173 N.C. App. 620 (2005).
- Time imprisoned as confinement in response to violation (CRV). G.S. 15A-1344(d2).
- Time imprisoned as a "quick dip" under G.S. 15A-1343(a1)(3) or -1343.2.
- **DWI** Time spent as an inpatient at a state-operated or state-licensed treatment facility for the treatment of alcoholism or substance abuse, provided such treatment occurred after the commission of the offense for which the defendant is being sentenced. G.S. 20-179(k1).

Do *Not* Count for Jail Credit

- Time in custody on a pending charge while serving a sentence imposed for another offense. G.S. 15-196.1.
- Time spent under electronic house arrest. State v. Jarman, 140 N.C. App. 198 (2000).
- Time spent at a privately run residential treatment program. State v. Stephenson, 213 N.C. App. 621 (2011).
- When two or more consecutive sentences are activated upon revocation of probation, credit for time served on concurrent CRV periods shall be credited to only one sentence. G.S. 15-196.2.
- **DWI** The first 24 hours spent in jail pending trial. G.S. 20-179(p).

Notes

Multiple charges. When a defendant is detained on multiple charges and has shared jail credit applicable to all of them, the following rules apply. If the convictions are sentenced to run **concurrently**, each sentence is credited by as much of the time as was spent in custody on each charge. If the convictions are sentenced to run **consecutively**, shared credit is applied against only one sentence. G.S. 15-196.2.

Special probation. When imposing special probation (a split sentence), the judge has discretion to order credit for any pretrial confinement to either the active portion of the split sentence or to the suspended sentence of imprisonment. G.S. 15A-1351(a).

`DWI` **Jail credit.** If a defendant sentenced under G.S. 20-179 is ordered to serve 48 hours or more or has 48 hours or more remaining on a term of imprisonment, he or she must be required to serve 48 continuous hours of imprisonment to be given credit. Credit for jail time may only be awarded hour for hour for time actually served. G.S. 20-179(s).

Sentence Reduction Credits

A defendant serving an active term of imprisonment may reduce his or her maximum sentence by working or participating in programming in prison. By Division of Adult Correction and Juvenile Justice (DACJJ) policy, **earned time** credit is awarded at 3, 6, or 9 days per month, depending on the nature of the work or program. A defendant may also accrue **meritorious time** for exemplary acts, working overtime, working in inclement weather, and other achievements. In no case may the defendant's sentence be reduced below the minimum term of imprisonment. A misdemeanant may reduce his or her sentence by up to 4 days per month through earned time and credit for work or educational programming. G.S. 15A-1340.20(d); 162-60. A term of special probation (a split sentence) may not be reduced by any sentence reduction credit. G.S. 148-13(f).

`DWI` By DAC regulation, DWI inmates are awarded good time at the rate of 1 day deducted from their prison or jail term for each day they spend in custody without a conviction through the Disciplinary Process of a violation of inmate conduct rules—which generally results in an inmate's sentence being cut in half. A defendant sentenced under G.S. 20-179 is eligible for good time credit regardless of the place of confinement. Good time may not be used to reduce an inmate's sentence below the mandatory minimum period of imprisonment for his or her level of DWI. G.S. 20-179(r). The prison system does not award good time to Aggravated Level One DWI sentences.

DWI Parole

`DWI` Defendants sentenced to a term of imprisonment for a conviction sentenced under G.S. 20-179—other than defendants sentenced at Aggravated Level One—are eligible for parole. G.S. 15A-1371.

If the sentence includes a minimum term of imprisonment, the person is eligible for release on parole upon completion of the minimum term or one-fifth the maximum penalty allowed by law, whichever is less, subject to the limitations below. If no minimum sentence is imposed for a prisoner serving an active term of imprisonment for a conviction of impaired driving, the person is eligible for release on parole at any time, subject to the limitations below. Good time credit reduces the term that must expire before a defendant becomes eligible for release on parole. Because good time credit is awarded day for day, the time that must expire before a defendant is parole-eligible effectively is halved. G.S. 15A-1355(c). Limitations on DWI parole:

- A defendant may not be released on parole until he or she has served the mandatory minimum term of imprisonment. G.S. 20-179(p).
- To be released on parole, a defendant must have obtained a substance abuse assessment and have completed any recommended treatment or training program or must be paroled into a residential treatment program. G.S. 20-179(p).

In addition to the rules above, a defendant serving a sentence of imprisonment of not less than 30 days nor as great as 18 months under G.S. 20-179 may be released on parole after serving one-third of the maximum sentence as provided in G.S. 15A-1371(g).

DNA Sample

The court must, under G.S. 15A-266.4, order the defendant to provide a DNA sample as a condition of the sentence for defendants convicted of:

- Any felony.
- Assault on a handicapped person (G.S. 14-32.1).
- Stalking (G.S. 14-277.3A).
- Cyberstalking (G.S. 14-196.3).
- Any offense requiring registration as a sex offender (G.S. 14-208.6).

See **APPENDIX F**, Crimes Requiring Sex Offender Registration.

Diversions

Deferred Prosecution

Statutory deferred prosecution. The district attorney may defer prosecution for certain defendants charged with a misdemeanor or a Class H or Class I felony as provided in G.S. 15A-1341(a1). The defendant may be placed on probation for up to two years.

Before placing a defendant on deferred prosecution probation, the court must find that:

1. Prosecution has been deferred pursuant to a written agreement,
2. Each known victim has been notified and given an opportunity to be heard,
3. The defendant has not been convicted of any felony or misdemeanor involving moral turpitude,
4. The defendant has not previously been placed on probation, and
5. The defendant is unlikely to commit another offense other than a Class 3 misdemeanor.

Use form AOC-CR-610.

Drug Treatment Court deferred prosecution. Eligible defendants may, with court approval, be placed on probation if the district attorney defers prosecution to allow the defendant to participate in the Drug Treatment Court Program. G.S. 15A-1341(a2).

Informal deferred prosecution. The district attorney may, in his or her discretion, have a deferred prosecution program, with eligibility and conditions dictated by local practice. Informal arrangements should not include probation.

Conditional Discharge

A conditional discharge allows a defendant who pleads guilty or is found guilty to be placed on probation without entry of judgment. If the defendant succeeds on probation, the court dismisses the conviction. If the defendant fails, the court enters judgment and sentences the defendant. Several statutes allow for conditional discharge for different types of offenses in North Carolina. The maximum period of probation for a conditional discharge is generally 2 years. G.S. 15A-1342(a).

Conditional Discharge under G.S. 15A-1341(a4)

Certain defendants who plead guilty or are found guilty of any Class H or Class I felony or a misdemeanor other than impaired driving may, on joint motion of the defendant and prosecution, be placed on conditional discharge probation. Before placing a defendant on conditional discharge probation under G.S. 15A-1341(a4), the court must find that:

1. Each known victim has been notified and given an opportunity to be heard,
2. The defendant has not been convicted of any felony or misdemeanor involving moral turpitude,
3. The defendant has not previously been placed on probation, and
4. The defendant is unlikely to commit another offense other than a Class 3 misdemeanor.

Use form AOC-CR-632D.

G.S. 90-96

Two similar but distinct conditional discharges are described in G.S. 90-96, subsection (a) and subsection (a1). Both apply to eligible defendants who plead guilty to or are found guilty of the following offenses:

- Misdemeanor possession of a controlled substance in Schedules I–VI
- Felony possession of a controlled substance under G.S. 90-95(a)(3)
- Misdemeanor possession of drug paraphernalia under G.S. 90-113.22 or marijuana drug paraphernalia under G.S. 90-113.22A

  Eligible defendants are those who:

- Have no prior felony convictions of any type,
- Have no prior convictions under Article 5 of G.S. Chapter 90, and
- Have never received a prior discharge and dismissal under G.S. 90-96 or 90-113.14.

Subsection (a). Conditional discharge under G.S. 90-96(a) is mandatory for consenting, eligible defendants unless the court determines, with a written finding and with the consent of the district attorney, that the defendant is inappropriate for a conditional discharge for factors related to the offense. Probation under G.S. 90-96(a) may include conditions in the court's discretion. Use form AOC-CR-619D.

Subsection (a1). Conditional discharge under G.S. 90-96(a1) is within the discretion of the court for eligible defendants. For the purpose of determining eligibility under subsection (a1), prior convictions and prior conditional discharges that occurred more than seven years before the date of the current offense do not count. Probation under subsection (a1) must be for at least one year and shall include a condition requiring the defendant to enroll in and complete Drug Education School within 150 days of being placed on probation, unless no school is available or there are other extenuating circumstances. Use form AOC-CR-627D.

Prostitution

Conditional discharge is mandatory for consenting first offenders of prostitution. The probation shall be for 12 months and shall require the conditions listed in G.S. 14-204(b). Use form AOC-CR-628D.

Drug Treatment Court

The court may, without entering a judgment of guilt and with the consent of the defendant, place a convicted defendant on conditional discharge probation to participate in the Drug Treatment Court Program. G.S. 15A-1341(a5). Use form AOC-CR-633D.

Gang offenders

Certain first-time gang offenders under the age of 18 at the time of their offense are, with their consent, eligible for conditional discharge as provided in G.S. 14-50.29. The probation must be for at least 1 year. Use for AOC-CR-621D.

Communicating a threat of mass violence on educational property or at a place of religious worship

G.S. 14-277.8 describes a conditional discharge for defendants under age 20 with no prior convictions for any felony or misdemeanor who are convicted of communicating a threat of mass violence under G.S. 14-277.6 (educational property) or 14-277.7 (place of religious worship). Probation imposed under that provision must be supervised for not less than one year and must include the conditions listed in G.S. 14-277.8(b). The law applies to offenses committed on or after December 1, 2018.

Prayer For Judgment Continued (PJC)

A prayer for judgment continued (PJC) is permissible for any defendant who is found guilty or pleads guilty to any crime except:

- Impaired driving (*In re* Greene, 297 N.C. 305 (1979));
- Solicitation of prostitution (G.S. 14-205.1(a));
- Speeding in excess of 25 m.p.h. over the posted limit (G.S. 20-141(p)); and
- Passing a stopped school bus (G.S. 20-217(e)).

For Class B1–E felonies committed on or after December 1, 2012, the court shall not dispose of a case by ordering a PJC that exceeds 12 months. The court may continue the initial order for an additional period not to exceed 12 months in the interest of justice. G.S. 15A-1331.2.

A PJC is converted into a judgment when it includes conditions that amount to punishment. Conditions not amounting to punishment include payment of costs, G.S. 15A-101(4a), and a requirement to obey the law, State v. Brown, 110 N.C. App. 658 (1993).

Work Release

Work release is the temporary release of a sentenced inmate to work on a job in the free community, outside the jail or prison, for which the inmate is paid by the outside employer.

Felonies

When a person is given an active sentence for a felony, the court may recommend work release. G.S. 15A-1351(f). The prison system makes the ultimate decision of whether and when to grant work release. G.S. 148-33.1. The court shall consider recommending to the Secretary of Public Safety that any restitution be made out of the defendant's work release earnings. G.S. 15A-1340.36.

Misdemeanors

When a person is given an active sentence for a misdemeanor, the judge may recommend work release. With the consent of the defendant, the judge may order work release. G.S. 15A-1351(f). When ordering work release, the judge must indicate the date the work is to begin, the place of confinement, a provision that work release terminates if the offender loses his or her job, and a determination about the disbursement of earnings, including how much should be paid to the assigned custodian for the costs of the prisoner's keep. G.S. 15A-1353(f); 148-33.1(f). The court may commit the defendant to a specific jail or prison facility to facilitate an ordered work release arrangement, as provided in G.S. 15A-1352(d).

Probationary Cases

The judge should not make any recommendation on work release when placing a defendant on probation; that recommendation should be made, if at all, upon revocation of probation. G.S. 148-33.1(i).

Obtaining Additional Information for Sentencing

Presentence Investigation

In any case, the court may order a probation officer to make a presentence investigation of the defendant. G.S. 15A-1332(b). To accommodate rotation, a judge who orders a presentence report may direct that the sentencing hearing in the case be held before him or her in another district during or after the session in which the defendant was convicted. G.S. 15A-1334(c).

`DWI` When a person has been convicted of an offense involving impaired driving, the court may, unless the person objects, request a presentence investigation to determine whether the person would benefit from treatment for habitual use of alcohol or drugs. G.S. 20-179.1.

Presentence Commitment for Study

Defendants charged with or convicted of any felony or a Class A1 or Class 1 misdemeanor may, with the defendant's consent, be committed to prison for up to 90 days for diagnostic study. G.S. 15A-1332(c). Contact the Division of Adult Correction and Juvenile Justice (DACJJ) Diagnostic Services Branch at 984-255-6125 to make arrangements. The Diagnostic Services Branch will provide the location and date of the evaluation. Use form AOC-CR-232.

Probationary Sentences

Probation is a suspended sentence of imprisonment that requires compliance with conditions set by the court. There are two types of probationary sentences, Intermediate punishment and Community punishment. When the court imposes a probationary sentence, it must indicate the type of probation, the length of the probation period, the conditions of probation, and whether or not delegated authority applies.

Types of Probation

Intermediate Punishment (G.S. 15A-1340.11(6))

Intermediate punishment requires that the court suspend the sentence of imprisonment and impose SUPERVISED probation.

For Offenses Committed on or after December 1, 2011

An Intermediate punishment is supervised probation that MAY include drug treatment court, a split sentence, or other conditions in the discretion of the court, including any of the "community and intermediate probation conditions" set out in G.S. 15A-1343(a1).

For Offenses Committed before December 1, 2011

An Intermediate punishment is supervised probation that MUST include at least one of the following six conditions:

1. Special probation (split sentence)
2. Residential program
3. Electronic house arrest
4. Intensive supervision
5. Day-reporting center
6. Drug treatment court

Special Probation (Split Sentence) (G.S. 15A-1351(a))

Special probation, often referred to as a split sentence, is a term of probation that includes a period or periods of incarceration. The total of all periods of special probation confinement may not exceed one-fourth the maximum imposed sentence. Imprisonment may be in prison or a designated jail or treatment facility, as provided in **APPENDIX G** , Place of Confinement Chart. If confinement is in the jail, the court may order the defendant to pay a $40 per day jail fee. G.S. 7A-313. Imprisonment may be for noncontinuous periods, such as weekends; noncontinuous imprisonment may be served only in a jail or treatment facility, not in prison. No confinement other than an activated sentence may be required beyond two years of conviction.

Community Punishment (G.S. 15A-1340.11(2))

Community punishment requires that the court suspend the sentence of imprisonment and impose SUPERVISED or UNSUPERVISED probation. A Community punishment also may consist of a fine only.

For Offenses Committed on or after December 1, 2011

A Community punishment is a non-active punishment that does not include drug treatment court or special probation but that may include any of the "community and intermediate probation conditions" set out in G.S. 15A-1343(a1).

For Offenses Committed before December 1, 2011

A Community punishment is a non-active punishment that does not include any of the six conditions set out above that formerly made a sentence an Intermediate punishment.

DWI Probation

DWI The distinctions between Community and Intermediate punishment do not apply to probationary sentences under G.S. 20-179. However, the following DWI-specific rules apply.

Special Probation (Split Sentence) for DWI (G.S. 15A-1351(a))

The total of all periods of confinement imposed as special probation under G.S. 20-179 may not exceed one-fourth the maximum authorized sentence for the level at which the defendant was punished. G.S. 15A-1351(a). The judge may order that a term of imprisonment imposed as a condition of special probation be served as an inpatient in a facility operated or licensed by the State for the treatment of alcoholism or substance abuse where the defendant has been accepted for admission or commitment as an in-patient. The defendant must bear the expense of any treatment unless the judge orders that the costs be absorbed by the State.

Preference for Unsupervised Probation (G.S. 20-179(r))

Unless the judge makes specific findings in the record about the need for probation supervision, a person sentenced at Levels Three through Five must be placed on unsupervised probation if he or she

- has no impaired driving convictions in the seven years preceding the current offense date and
- has been assessed and completed any recommended treatment.

If a judge places a convicted impaired driver on supervised probation under this subsection based on a finding that supervised probation is necessary, the judge must authorize the probation officer to transfer the defendant to unsupervised probation after he or she completes any ordered community service and pays any fines.

Continuous Alcohol Monitoring (CAM)

In addition to the requirements set out in the DWI sentencing grids, the following rules apply to continuous alcohol monitoring (CAM) ordered as part of a DWI sentence for an offense committed on or after December 1, 2012.

- A judge may order as a condition of probation for any level of punishment under G.S. 20-179 that the defendant abstain from alcohol consumption, as verified by CAM. G.S. 20-179(k2).
- A judge may authorize a probation officer to require a defendant to submit to CAM for assessment purposes if the defendant is required, as a condition of probation, not to consume alcohol and the probation officer believes the defendant is consuming alcohol. If the probation officer orders the defendant to submit to CAM pursuant to this provision, the defendant must bear the costs of CAM. G.S. 20-179(k3).
- A court may not impose CAM pursuant to G.S. 20-179(k2) or (k3) if it finds good cause that the defendant should not be required to pay the costs of CAM, unless the local governmental entity responsible for the incarceration of the defendant in the local confinement facility agrees to pay the costs of the system.

Period of Probation

When a judge suspends a sentence of imprisonment and places a defendant on probation, the judge must decide how long the period of probation will be. The permissible length of the period of probation is governed by statute (it does not flow from the length of the suspended sentence of imprisonment).

Under G.S. 15A-1343.2(d), the original period of probation in a case sentenced under Structured Sentencing must fall within the following limits:

Offense Class	Community Punishment	Intermediate Punishment
Misdemeanant	6 to 18 months	12 to 24 months
Felon	12 to 30 months	18 to 36 months

The court may depart from these ranges with a finding that a longer or shorter period is required. The maximum permissible period is 5 years.

DWI The permissible length of probation in a DWI case is 5 years, and no special findings are required to impose a probationary sentence of that length.

The maximum period of probation for a deferred prosecution or conditional discharge is 2 years. G.S. 15A-1342(a).

Conditions of Probation

The sentencing judge has broad discretion to shape the conditions of the defendant's probation. Conditions fall into different categories, some of which apply by default and some which may be added by the court, as indicated in the lists below.

Note: The numbering of the conditions in this handbook mirrors the numbering used in the referenced General Statute sections. Omitted numbers indicate repealed conditions.

Regular Conditions (G.S. 15A-1343(b))

Regular conditions of probation apply to each defendant placed on supervised probation unless the presiding judge specifically exempts the defendant from one or more of the conditions in open court and in the judgment of the court. Regular conditions are as follows:

1. Commit no criminal offense in any jurisdiction.
*2. Remain within the jurisdiction of the court unless granted written permission to leave by the court or the defendant's probation officer.
*3. Report as directed by the court or the defendant's probation officer to the officer at reasonable times and places and in a reasonable manner; permit the officer to visit the probationer at reasonable times; answer all reasonable inquiries by the officer and obtain prior approval from the officer for, and notify the officer of, any change in address or employment.
*3a. Not abscond, by willfully avoiding supervision or by willfully making the defendant's whereabouts unknown to the supervising probation officer. [*Offenses committed on/after 12/1/2011.*]
4. Satisfy child support and other family obligations as required by the court. If the court requires the payment of child support, the amount of the payments shall be determined as provided in G.S. 50-13.4(c).
5. Possess no firearm, explosive device, or other deadly weapon listed in G.S. 14-269 without the written permission of the court.
*6. Pay a supervision fee.
7. Remain gainfully and suitably employed or faithfully pursue a course of study or of vocational training that will equip the probationer for suitable employment. A defendant pursuing a course of study or of vocational training shall abide by all of the rules of the institution providing the education or training, and the probation

officer shall forward a copy of the probation judgment to that institution and request to be notified of any violations of institutional rules by the defendant.

*8. Notify the probation officer if the probationer fails to obtain or retain satisfactory employment.

 9. Pay the costs of court and any fine ordered by the court and make restitution or reparation as provided in G.S. 15A-1343(d).

10. Pay the State of North Carolina for the costs of appointed counsel, public defender, or appellate defender to represent the defendant in the case(s) for which he or she was placed on probation.

12. Attend and complete an abuser treatment program if (i) the court finds that the defendant is responsible for acts of domestic violence and (ii) there is a program, approved by the Domestic Violence Commission, reasonably available to the defendant, unless the court finds that such would not be in the best interests of justice.

*13. Submit at reasonable times to warrantless searches by a probation officer of the probationer's person and of the probationer's vehicle and premises while the probationer is present, for purposes directly related to the probation supervision, but the probationer may not be required to submit to any other search that would otherwise be unlawful. [*Offenses committed on/after 12/1/2009.*]

*14. Submit to warrantless searches by a law enforcement officer of the probationer's person and of the probationer's vehicle, upon a reasonable suspicion that the probationer is engaged in criminal activity or is in possession of a firearm, explosive device, or other deadly weapon listed in G.S. 14-269 without written permission of the court. [*Offenses committed on/after 12/1/2009.*]

*15. Not use, possess, or control any illegal drug or controlled substance unless it has been prescribed for him or her by a licensed physician and is in the original container with the prescription number affixed on it; not knowingly associate with any known or previously convicted users, possessors, or sellers of any such illegal drugs or controlled substances; and not knowingly be present at or frequent any place where such illegal drugs or controlled substances are sold, kept, or used. [*Offenses committed on/after 12/1/2009.*]

*16. Supply a breath, urine, or blood specimen for analysis of the possible presence of prohibited drugs or alcohol when instructed by the defendant's probation officer for purposes directly related to the probation supervision. If the results of the analysis are positive, the probationer may be required to reimburse the Division of Adult Correction and Juvenile Justice (DACJJ) of the Department of Public Safety for the actual costs of drug or alcohol screening and testing. [*Offenses committed on/after 12/1/2011.*]

*17. Waive all rights relating to extradition proceedings if taken into custody outside of this state for failing to comply with the conditions imposed by the court upon a felony conviction. [*Offenses committed on/after 12/1/2016.*]

18. Submit to the taking of digitized photographs, including photographs of the probationer's face, scars, marks, and tattoos, to be included in the probationer's records. [*Offenses committed on/after 12/1/2016.*]

---

   * Does not apply to defendants on unsupervised probation.

If ordered to special probation, the defendant is required to obey the rules and regulations of DACJJ governing the conduct of inmates while imprisoned and report to a probation officer in the State of North Carolina within seventy-two hours of discharge from the active term of imprisonment.

Special Conditions (G.S. 15A-1343(b1))

The court may require that the defendant comply with one or more of the following special conditions:

1. Undergo available medical or psychiatric treatment and remain in a specified institution if required for that purpose. Notwithstanding the provisions of G.S. 15A-1344(e) or any other provision of law, the defendant may be required to participate in such treatment for its duration regardless of the length of the suspended sentence imposed.

2. Attend or reside in a facility providing rehabilitation, counseling, treatment, social skills, or employment training, instruction, recreation, or residence for persons on probation.

2b. Participate in and successfully complete a Drug Treatment Court Program pursuant to Article 62 of Chapter 7A of the General Statutes.

2c. Abstain from alcohol consumption and submit to continuous alcohol monitoring when alcohol dependency or chronic abuse has been identified by a substance abuse assessment.

3. Submit to imprisonment required for special probation under G.S. 15A-1351(a) or -1344(e).

3c. Remain at his or her residence. The court, in the sentencing order, may authorize the offender to leave the offender's residence for employment, counseling, a course of study, vocational training, or other specific purposes and may modify that authorization. The probation officer may authorize the offender to leave the offender's residence for specific purposes not authorized in the court order upon approval of the probation officer's supervisor. The offender shall be required to wear a device which permits the supervising agency to monitor the offender's compliance with the condition electronically and to pay a fee for the device as specified in G.S. 15A-1343(c2).

4. Surrender his or her driver's license to the clerk of superior court and not operate a motor vehicle for a period specified by the court.

5. Compensate the Department of Environmental Quality or the North Carolina Wildlife Resources Commission, as the case may be, for the replacement costs of any marine and estuarine resources or any wildlife resources which were taken, injured, removed, harmfully altered, damaged, or destroyed as a result of a criminal offense of which the defendant was convicted. If any investigation is required by officers or agents of the Department of Environmental Quality or the Wildlife Resources Commission in determining the extent of the destruction of resources involved, the court may include compensation of the agency for investigative costs as a condition of probation. The court may also include, as a condition of probation, compensation of an agency for any reward paid for information leading to the arrest and conviction of the offender. This subdivision does not apply in any case governed by G.S. 143-215.3(a)(7).

6. Perform community or reparation service under the supervision of the Section of Community Corrections of the Division of Adult Correction and Juvenile Justice (DACJJ) and pay the fee required by G.S. 143B-708.

8a. Purchase the least expensive annual statewide license or combination of licenses to hunt, trap, or fish listed in G.S. 113-270.2, -270.3, -270.5, -271, -272, and -272.2 that would be required to engage lawfully in the specific activity or activities in which the defendant was engaged and which constitute the basis of the offense or offenses of which he or she was convicted.

9. If the offense is one in which there is evidence of physical, mental, or sexual abuse of a minor, the court should encourage the minor and the minor's parents or custodians to participate in rehabilitative treatment and may order the defendant to pay the cost of such treatment.

9b. Any or all of the following conditions relating to criminal gangs as defined in G.S. 14-50.16A(1): Not knowingly associate with any known criminal gang members and not knowingly be present at or frequent any place or location where criminal gangs gather or where criminal gang activity is known to occur; not wear clothes, jewelry, signs, symbols, or any paraphernalia readily identifiable as associated with or used by a criminal gang; not initiate or participate in any contact with any individual who was or may be a witness against or victim of the defendant or the defendant's criminal gang.

9c. Participate in any Project Safe Neighborhood activities as directed by the probation officer.

10. Satisfy any other conditions determined by the court to be reasonably related to his or her rehabilitation.

Community and Intermediate Conditions (G.S. 15A-1343(a1))

For Structured Sentencing offenses committed on or after December 1, 2011, the court may include any one or more of the following conditions as part of a Community or Intermediate punishment:

1. House arrest with electronic monitoring.
2. Perform community service and pay the fee prescribed by law for this supervision.
3. Submit to a period or periods of confinement in a local confinement facility for a total of no more than 6 days per month during any three separate months during the period of probation. The 6 days per month confinement provided for in this subdivision may only be imposed as 2-day or 3-day consecutive periods. When a defendant is on probation for multiple judgments, confinement periods imposed under this subdivision shall run concurrently and may total no more than 6 days per month.
4. Substance abuse assessment, monitoring, or treatment.
4a. Abstain from alcohol consumption and submit to continuous alcohol monitoring when alcohol dependency or chronic abuse has been identified by a substance abuse assessment. [*Offenses committed on/after 12/1/2012.*]
5. Participation in an educational or vocational skills development program, including an evidence-based program.
6. Submission to satellite-based monitoring, pursuant to Part 5 of Article 27A of Chapter 14 of the General Statutes, if the defendant is described by G.S. 14-208.40(a)(2).

Intermediate Conditions (G.S. 15A-1343(b4))

For offenses committed on or after December 1, 2009, the following conditions of probation apply to each defendant subject to Intermediate punishment, unless the court specifically exempts the defendant from one or more of the conditions in its judgment or order:

1. If required in the discretion of the defendant's probation officer, perform community service under the supervision of the Section of Community Corrections of the Division of Adult Correction and Juvenile Justice (DACJJ), Department of Public Safety and pay the fee required by G.S. 143B-708.
2. Not use, possess, or control alcohol.
3. Remain within the county of residence unless granted written permission to leave by the court or the defendant's probation officer.
4. Participate in any evaluation, counseling, treatment, or educational program as directed by the probation officer, keeping all appointments and abiding by the rules, regulations, and direction of each program.

Sex Offender Conditions (G.S. 15A-1343(b2))

A defendant who has been convicted of a reportable sex crime or an offense that involves the physical, mental, or sexual abuse of a minor must be made subject to the following conditions. These defendants may not be placed on unsupervised probation.

1. Register as required by G.S. 14-208.7 if the offense is a reportable conviction as defined by G.S. 14-208.6(4).
2. Participate in such evaluation and treatment as is necessary to complete a prescribed course of psychiatric, psychological, or other rehabilitative treatment as ordered by the court.
3. Not communicate with, be in the presence of, or found in or on the premises of the victim of the offense.
4. Not reside in a household with any minor child if the offense is one in which there is evidence of sexual abuse of a minor.
5. Not reside in a household with any minor child if the offense is one in which there is evidence of physical or mental abuse of a minor, unless the court expressly finds that it is unlikely that the defendant's harmful or abusive conduct will recur and that it would be in the minor child's best interest to allow the probationer to reside in the same household with a minor child.
6. Satisfy any other conditions determined by the court to be reasonably related to his or her rehabilitation.
7. Submit to satellite-based monitoring pursuant to Part 5 of Article 27A of Chapter 14 of the General Statutes, if the defendant is described by G.S. 14-208.40(a)(1).
8. Submit to satellite-based monitoring pursuant to Part 5 of Article 27A of Chapter 14 of the General Statutes, if the defendant described by G.S. 14-208.40(a)(2) and the Division of Adult Correction and Juvenile Justice (DACJJ), based on its risk assessment program, recommends that the defendant submit to the highest possible level of supervision and monitoring.
9. Submit at reasonable times to warrantless searches by a probation officer of the probationer's person and of the probationer's vehicle and premises while the probationer is present, for purposes specified by the court and reasonably related to the probation supervision, but the probationer may not be required to submit to any other search that would otherwise be unlawful. For purposes of this subdivision, warrantless searches of the probationer's computer or other electronic mechanism which may contain electronic data shall be considered reasonably related to the probation supervision. Whenever the warrantless search consists of testing for the presence of illegal drugs, the probationer may also be required to reimburse DACJJ for the actual cost of drug screening and drug testing, if the results are positive.

Delegated Authority (G.S. 15A-1343.2)

Delegated authority applies only to crimes sentenced under Structured Sentencing. Thus, it does not apply to DWI probationers sentenced under G.S. 20-179. Unless the presiding judge specifically finds in the judgment of the court that delegation is not appropriate, a probation officer may require an offender to do any of the following:

Community Punishment Cases

1. Perform up to 20 hours of community service and pay the fee prescribed by law for this supervision.
2. Report to the offender's probation officer on a frequency to be determined by the officer.
3. Submit to substance abuse assessment, monitoring, or treatment.
4. Submit to house arrest with electronic monitoring. [*Offenses committed on/after 12/1/2011.*]

5. Submit to a period or periods of confinement in a local confinement facility for a total of no more than 6 days per month during any three separate months during the period of probation. The 6 days per month confinement provided for in this subdivision may only be imposed as 2-day or 3-day consecutive periods. [*Offenses committed on/after 12/1/2011.*]
6. Submit to a curfew which requires the offender to remain in a specified place for a specified period each day and wear a device that permits the offender's compliance with the condition to be monitored electronically. [*Offenses committed on/after 12/1/2011.*]
7. Participate in an educational or vocational skills development program, including an evidence-based program. [*Offenses committed on/after 12/1/2011.*]

Intermediate Punishment Cases

1. Perform up to 50 hours of community service and pay the fee prescribed by law for this supervision.
2. Submit to a curfew which requires the offender to remain in a specified place for a specified period each day and wear a device that permits the offender's compliance with the condition to be monitored electronically.
3. Submit to substance abuse assessment, monitoring, or treatment, including [*for offenses committed on/after 12/1/2012*] continuous alcohol monitoring when abstinence from alcohol consumption has been specified as a term of probation.
4. Participate in an educational or vocational skills development program, including an evidence-based program.
5. Submit to satellite-based monitoring if the defendant is described by G.S. 14-208.40(a)(2).
6. Submit to a period or periods of confinement in a local confinement facility for a total of no more than 6 days per month during any three separate months during the period of probation. The 6 days per month confinement provided for in this subdivision may only be imposed as 2-day or 3-day consecutive periods. [*Offenses committed on/after 12/1/2011.*]
7. Submit to house arrest with electronic monitoring. [*Offenses committed on/after 12/1/2011.*]
8. Report to the offender's probation officer on a frequency to be determined by the officer. [*Offenses committed on/after 12/1/2011.*]

The officer may impose the conditions listed above upon a determination that the offender has violated a court-imposed probation condition. For offenses on or after December 1, 2011, the officer may also impose any condition except jail confinement for defendants deemed to be high risk based on a risk assessment. Jail confinement may be ordered only in response to a violation, and only when the probationer waives his or her rights to a hearing and counsel.

Felony Offenses Committed on or after **October 1, 2013**
MINIMUM SENTENCES AND DISPOSITIONAL OPTIONS

OFFENSE CLASS	PRIOR RECORD LEVEL						DISPOSITION
	I 0–1 Pt	**II** 2–5 Pts	**III** 6–9 Pts	**IV** 10–13 Pts	**V** 14–17 Pts	**VI** 18+ Pts	
A Max. Death or Life w/o Parole	Death or Life without Parole Defendant under 18 at Time of Offense: Life with or without Parole						
B1 Max. Life w/o Parole	A 240–300 **192–240** 144–192	A 276–345 **221–276** 166–221	A 317–397 **254–317** 190–254	A 365–456 **292–365** 219–292	A Life w/o Parole **336–420** 252–336	A Life w/o Parole **386–483** 290–386	Aggravated **PRESUMPTIVE** Mitigated
B2 Max. 484 (532)	A ᴱᴹ 157–196 **125–157** 94–125	A ᴱᴹ 180–225 **144–180** 108–144	A 207–258 **165–207** 124–165	A 238–297 **190–238** 143–190	A 273–342 **219–273** 164–219	A 314–393 **251–314** 189–251	
C Max. 231 (279)	A ᴱᴹ 73–92 **58–73** 44–58	A ᴱᴹ 83–104 **67–83** 50–67	A 96–120 **77–96** 58–77	A 110–138 **88–110** 66–88	A 127–159 **101–127** 76–101	A 146–182 **117–146** 87–117	
D Max. 204 (252)	A ᴱᴹ 64–80 **51–64** ASR 38–51	A ᴱᴹ 73–92 **59–73** ASR 44–59	A 84–105 **67–84** ASR 51–67	A 97–121 **78–97** 58–78	A 111–139 **89–111** 67–89	A 128–160 **103–128** 77–103	
E Max. 88 (136)	I/A 25–31 **20–25** ASR 15–20	I/A 29–36 **23–29** ASR 17–23	A 33–41 **26–33** ASR 20–26	A 38–48 **30–38** ASR 23–30	A 44–55 **35–44** 26–35	A 50–63 **40–50** 30–40	
F Max. 59	I/A 16–20 **13–16** ASR 10–13	I/A 19–23 **15–19** ASR 11–15	I/A 21–27 **17–21** ASR 13–17	A 25–31 **20–25** ASR 15–20	A 28–36 **23–28** ASR 17–23	A 33–41 **26–33** 20–26	
G Max. 47	I/A 13–16 **10–13** ASR 8–10	I/A 14–18 **12–14** ASR 9–12	I/A 17–21 **13–17** ASR 10–13	I/A 19–24 **15–19** ASR 11–15	A 22–27 **17–22** ASR 13–17	A 25–31 **20–25** ASR 15–20	
H Max. 39	C/I/A 6–8 **5–6** 4–5	I/A 8–10 **6–8** ASR 4–6	I/A 10–12 **8–10** ASR 6–8	I/A 11–14 **9–11** ASR 7–9	I/A 15–19 **12–15** ASR 9–12	A 20–25 **16–20** ASR 12–16	
I Max. 24	C 6–8 **4–6** 3–4	C/I 6–8 **4–6** 3–4	I 6–8 **5–6** 4–5	I/A 8–10 **6–8** 4–6	I/A 9–11 **7–9** 5–7	I/A 10–12 **8–10** 6–8	

Note: Numbers shown are in months. The number shown below each offense class reflects the maximum possible sentence for that class of offense (the highest maximum sentence from the aggravated range in prior record level VI). The maximum sentence for a defendant convicted of a reportable Class B1 through E sex crime is indicated in parentheses.

A—Active Punishment
I—Intermediate Punishment
C—Community Punishment

ᴱᴹ **Extraordinary Mitigation** (possible eligibility). *See* page 10.

ASR **Advanced Supervised Release** (possible eligibility). *See* page 10.

MAXIMUM SENTENCES

The tables below show the maximum sentence that corresponds to each minimum sentence. For minimum sentences of 340 months or more, the maximum sentence is 120 percent of the minimum sentence, rounded to the next highest month, plus 12 additional months. G.S. 15A-1340.17(e1).

Sex Crimes: The maximum sentence for a Class B1 through E felony subject to the registration requirements of G.S. Chapter 14, Article 27A is 120 percent of the minimum sentence, rounded to the next highest month, plus 60 additional months, as indicated in parentheses below. G.S. 15A-1340.17(f).

FOR OFFENSE CLASSES B1 THROUGH E [Minimum Sentence ➜ Corresponding Maximum (*Sex Crimes*)]

15→30 (78)	56→80 (128)	97→129 (177)	138→178 (226)	179→227 (275)	220→276 (324)	261→326 (374)	302→375 (423)
16→32 (80)	57→81 (129)	98→130 (178)	139→179 (227)	180→228 (276)	221→278 (326)	262→327 (375)	303→376 (424)
17→33 (81)	58→82 (130)	99→131 (179)	140→180 (228)	181→230 (278)	222→279 (327)	263→328 (376)	304→377 (425)
18→34 (82)	59→83 (131)	100→132 (180)	141→182 (230)	182→231 (279)	223→280 (328)	264→329 (377)	305→378 (426)
19→35 (83)	60→84 (132)	101→134 (182)	142→183 (231)	183→232 (280)	224→281 (329)	265→330 (378)	306→380 (428)
20→36 (84)	61→86 (134)	102→135 (183)	143→184 (232)	184→233 (281)	225→282 (330)	266→332 (380)	307→381 (429)
21→38 (86)	62→87 (135)	103→136 (184)	144→185 (233)	185→234 (282)	226→284 (332)	267→333 (381)	308→382 (430)
22→39 (87)	63→88 (136)	104→137 (185)	145→186 (234)	186→236 (284)	227→285 (333)	268→334 (382)	309→383 (431)
23→40 (88)	64→89 (137)	105→138 (186)	146→188 (236)	187→237 (285)	228→286 (334)	269→335 (383)	310→384 (432)
24→41 (89)	65→90 (138)	106→140 (188)	147→189 (237)	188→238 (286)	229→287 (335)	270→336 (384)	311→386 (434)
25→42 (90)	66→92 (140)	107→141 (189)	148→190 (238)	189→239 (287)	230→288 (336)	271→338 (386)	312→387 (435)
26→44 (92)	67→93 (141)	108→142 (190)	149→191 (239)	190→240 (288)	231→290 (338)	272→339 (387)	313→388 (436)
27→45 (93)	68→94 (142)	109→143 (191)	150→192 (240)	191→242 (290)	232→291 (339)	273→340 (388)	314→389 (437)
28→46 (94)	69→95 (143)	110→144 (192)	151→194 (242)	192→243 (291)	233→292 (340)	274→341 (389)	315→390 (438)
29→47 (95)	70→96 (144)	111→146 (194)	152→195 (243)	193→244 (292)	234→293 (341)	275→342 (390)	316→392 (440)
30→48 (96)	71→98 (146)	112→147 (195)	153→196 (244)	194→245 (293)	235→294 (342)	276→344 (392)	317→393 (441)
31→50 (98)	72→99 (147)	113→148 (196)	154→197 (245)	195→246 (294)	236→296 (344)	277→345 (393)	318→394 (442)
32→51 (99)	73→100 (148)	114→149 (197)	155→198 (246)	196→248 (296)	237→297 (345)	278→346 (394)	319→395 (443)
33→52 (100)	74→101 (149)	115→150 (198)	156→200 (248)	197→249 (297)	238→298 (346)	279→347 (395)	320→396 (444)
34→53 (101)	75→102 (150)	116→152 (200)	157→201 (249)	198→250 (298)	239→299 (347)	280→348 (396)	321→398 (446)
35→54 (102)	76→104 (152)	117→153 (201)	158→202 (250)	199→251 (299)	240→300 (348)	281→350 (398)	322→399 (447)
36→56 (104)	77→105 (153)	118→154 (202)	159→203 (251)	200→252 (300)	241→302 (350)	282→351 (399)	323→400 (448)
37→57 (105)	78→106 (154)	119→155 (203)	160→204 (252)	201→254 (302)	242→303 (351)	283→352 (400)	324→401 (449)
38→58 (106)	79→107 (155)	120→156 (204)	161→206 (254)	202→255 (303)	243→304 (352)	284→353 (401)	325→402 (450)
39→59 (107)	80→108 (156)	121→158 (206)	162→207 (255)	203→256 (304)	244→305 (353)	285→354 (402)	326→404 (452)
40→60 (108)	81→110 (158)	122→159 (207)	163→208 (256)	204→257 (305)	245→306 (354)	286→356 (404)	327→405 (453)
41→62 (110)	82→111 (159)	123→160 (208)	164→209 (257)	205→258 (306)	246→308 (356)	287→357 (405)	328→406 (454)
42→63 (111)	83→112 (160)	124→161 (209)	165→210 (258)	206→260 (308)	247→309 (357)	288→358 (406)	329→407 (455)
43→64 (112)	84→113 (161)	125→162 (210)	166→212 (260)	207→261 (309)	248→310 (358)	289→359 (407)	330→408 (456)
44→65 (113)	85→114 (162)	126→164 (212)	167→213 (261)	208→262 (310)	249→311 (359)	290→360 (408)	331→410 (458)
45→66 (114)	86→116 (164)	127→165 (213)	168→214 (262)	209→263 (311)	250→312 (360)	291→362 (410)	332→411 (459)
46→68 (116)	87→117 (165)	128→166 (214)	169→215 (263)	210→264 (312)	251→314 (362)	292→363 (411)	333→412 (460)
47→69 (117)	88→118 (166)	129→167 (215)	170→216 (264)	211→266 (314)	252→315 (363)	293→364 (412)	334→413 (461)
48→70 (118)	89→119 (167)	130→168 (216)	171→218 (266)	212→267 (315)	253→316 (364)	294→365 (413)	335→414 (462)
49→71 (119)	90→120 (168)	131→170 (218)	172→219 (267)	213→268 (316)	254→317 (365)	295→366 (414)	336→416 (464)
50→72 (120)	91→122 (170)	132→171 (219)	173→220 (268)	214→269 (317)	255→318 (366)	296→368 (416)	337→417 (465)
51→74 (122)	92→123 (171)	133→172 (220)	174→221 (269)	215→270 (318)	256→320 (368)	297→369 (417)	338→418 (466)
52→75 (123)	93→124 (172)	134→173 (221)	175→222 (270)	216→272 (320)	257→321 (369)	298→370 (418)	339→419 (467)
53→76 (124)	94→125 (173)	135→174 (222)	176→224 (272)	217→273 (321)	258→322 (370)	299→371 (419)	
54→77 (125)	95→126 (174)	136→176 (224)	177→225 (273)	218→274 (322)	259→323 (371)	300→372 (420)	
55→78 (126)	96→128 (176)	137→177 (225)	178→226 (274)	219→275 (323)	260→324 (372)	301→374 (422)	

FOR OFFENSE CLASSES F THROUGH I [Minimum Sentence ➜ Corresponding Maximum]

3→13	9→20	15→27	21→35	27→42	33→49	39→56	45→63
4→14	10→21	16→29	22→36	28→43	34→50	40→57	46→65
5→15	11→23	17→30	23→37	29→44	35→51	41→59	47→66
6→17	12→24	18→31	24→38	30→45	36→53	42→60	48→67
7→18	13→25	19→32	25→39	31→47	37→54	43→61	49→68
8→19	14→26	20→33	26→41	32→48	38→55	44→62	

Length of Probation Period

The original period of probation for a felony sentenced under Structured Sentencing must fall within the following limits:

- Community—12 to 30 months
- Intermediate—18 to 36 months

The court may depart from those ranges with a finding that a longer or shorter period is required. The maximum permissible period with a finding is 5 years. G.S. 15A-1343.2.

Post-Release Supervision

Class F–I felony—9 months
Class B1–E felony—12 months
Crimes requiring sex offender registration—5 years

Fines

Any felony sentence may include a fine. Unless otherwise provided for a specific offense, the amount of the fine is in the discretion of the court. G.S. 15A-1340.17(b).

Felony Offenses Committed **December 1, 2011**, through **September 30, 2013**
MINIMUM SENTENCES AND DISPOSITIONAL OPTIONS

OFFENSE CLASS	PRIOR RECORD LEVEL						DISPOSITION
	I 0–1 Pt	**II** 2–5 Pts	**III** 6–9 Pts	**IV** 10–13 Pts	**V** 14–17 Pts	**VI** 18+ Pts	
A Max. Death or Life w/o Parole	Death or Life without Parole — Defendant under 18 at Time of Offense: Life with or without Parole						
B1 Max. Life w/o Parole	A	A	A	A	A	A	
	240–300	276–345	317–397	365–456	Life w/o Parole	Life w/o Parole	Aggravated
	192–240	**221–276**	**254–317**	**292–365**	**336–420**	**386–483**	**PRESUMPTIVE**
	144–192	166–221	190–254	219–292	252–336	290–386	Mitigated
B2 Max. 484 (532)	A ᴱᴹ	A ᴱᴹ	A	A	A	A	
	157–196	180–225	207–258	238–297	273–342	314–393	
	125–157	**144–180**	**165–207**	**190–238**	**219–273**	**251–314**	
	94–125	108–144	124–165	143–190	164–219	189–251	
C Max. 231 (279)	A ᴱᴹ	A ᴱᴹ	A	A	A	A	
	73–92	83–104	96–120	110–138	127–159	146–182	
	58–73	**67–83**	**77–96**	**88–110**	**101–127**	**117–146**	
	44–58	50–67	58–77	66–88	76–101	87–117	
D Max. 204 (252)	A ᴱᴹ	A ᴱᴹ	A	A	A	A	
	64–80	73–92	84–105	97–121	111–139	128–160	
	51–64	**59–73**	**67–84**	**78–97**	**89–111**	**103–128**	
	ᴬˢᴿ 38–51	ᴬˢᴿ 44–59	ᴬˢᴿ 51–67	58–78	67–89	77–103	
E Max. 88 (136)	I/A	I/A	A	A	A	A	
	25–31	29–36	33–41	38–48	44–55	50–63	
	20–25	**23–29**	**26–33**	**30–38**	**35–44**	**40–50**	
	ᴬˢᴿ 15–20	ᴬˢᴿ 17–23	ᴬˢᴿ 20–26	ᴬˢᴿ 23–30	26–35	30–40	
F Max. 59	I/A	I/A	I/A	A	A	A	
	16–20	19–23	21–27	25–31	28–36	33–41	
	13–16	**15–19**	**17–21**	**20–25**	**23–28**	**26–33**	
	ᴬˢᴿ 10–13	ᴬˢᴿ 11–15	ᴬˢᴿ 13–17	ᴬˢᴿ 15–20	ᴬˢᴿ 17–23	20–26	
G Max. 47	I/A	I/A	I/A	I/A	A	A	
	13–16	14–18	17–21	19–24	22–27	25–31	
	10–13	**12–14**	**13–17**	**15–19**	**17–22**	**20–25**	
	ᴬˢᴿ 8–10	ᴬˢᴿ 9–12	ᴬˢᴿ 10–13	ᴬˢᴿ 11–15	ᴬˢᴿ 13–17	ᴬˢᴿ 15–20	
H Max. 39	C/I/A	I/A	I/A	I/A	I/A	A	
	6–8	8–10	10–12	11–14	15–19	20–25	
	5–6	**6–8**	**8–10**	**9–11**	**12–15**	**16–20**	
	ᴬˢᴿ 4–5	ᴬˢᴿ 4–6	ᴬˢᴿ 6–8	ᴬˢᴿ 7–9	ᴬˢᴿ 9–12	ᴬˢᴿ 12–16	
I Max. 24	C	C/I	I	I/A	I/A	I/A	
	6–8	6–8	6–8	8–10	9–11	10–12	
	4–6	**4–6**	**5–6**	**6–8**	**7–9**	**8–10**	
	3–4	3–4	4–5	4–6	5–7	6–8	

Note: Numbers shown are in months. The number shown below each offense class reflects the maximum possible sentence for that class of offense (the highest maximum sentence from the aggravated range in prior record level VI). The maximum sentence for a defendant convicted of a reportable Class B1 through E sex crime is indicated in parentheses.

A—Active Punishment
I—Intermediate Punishment
C—Community Punishment

ᴱᴹ **Extraordinary Mitigation** (possible eligibility). *See* page 10.

Advanced Supervised Release
ᴬˢᴿ (possible eligibility). *See* page 10.

MAXIMUM SENTENCES

The tables below show the maximum sentence that corresponds to each minimum sentence. For minimum sentences of 340 months or more, the maximum sentence is 120 percent of the minimum sentence, rounded to the next highest month, plus 12 additional months. G.S. 15A-1340.17(e1).

Sex Crimes: The maximum sentence for a Class B1 through E felony subject to the registration requirements of G.S. Chapter 14, Article 27A is 120 percent of the minimum sentence, rounded to the next highest month, plus 60 additional months, as indicated in parentheses below. G.S. 15A-1340.17(f).

FOR OFFENSE CLASSES B1 THROUGH E [Minimum Sentence → Corresponding Maximum (*Sex Crimes*)]

15→30 (78)	56→80 (128)	97→129 (177)	138→178 (226)	179→227 (275)	220→276 (324)	261→326 (374)	302→375 (423)
16→32 (80)	57→81 (129)	98→130 (178)	139→179 (227)	180→228 (276)	221→278 (326)	262→327 (375)	303→376 (424)
17→33 (81)	58→82 (130)	99→131 (179)	140→180 (228)	181→230 (278)	222→279 (327)	263→328 (376)	304→377 (425)
18→34 (82)	59→83 (131)	100→132 (180)	141→182 (230)	182→231 (279)	223→280 (328)	264→329 (377)	305→378 (426)
19→35 (83)	60→84 (132)	101→134 (182)	142→183 (231)	183→232 (280)	224→281 (329)	265→330 (378)	306→380 (428)
20→36 (84)	61→86 (134)	102→135 (183)	143→184 (232)	184→233 (281)	225→282 (330)	266→332 (380)	307→381 (429)
21→38 (86)	62→87 (135)	103→136 (184)	144→185 (233)	185→234 (282)	226→284 (332)	267→333 (381)	308→382 (430)
22→39 (87)	63→88 (136)	104→137 (185)	145→186 (234)	186→236 (284)	227→285 (333)	268→334 (382)	309→383 (431)
23→40 (88)	64→89 (137)	105→138 (186)	146→188 (236)	187→237 (285)	228→286 (334)	269→335 (383)	310→384 (432)
24→41 (89)	65→90 (138)	106→140 (188)	147→189 (237)	188→238 (286)	229→287 (335)	270→336 (384)	311→386 (434)
25→42 (90)	66→91 (140)	107→141 (189)	148→190 (238)	189→239 (287)	230→288 (336)	271→338 (386)	312→387 (435)
26→44 (92)	67→93 (141)	108→142 (190)	149→191 (239)	190→240 (288)	231→290 (338)	272→339 (387)	313→388 (436)
27→45 (93)	68→94 (142)	109→143 (191)	150→192 (240)	191→242 (290)	232→291 (339)	273→340 (388)	314→389 (437)
28→46 (94)	69→95 (143)	110→144 (192)	151→194 (242)	192→243 (291)	233→292 (340)	274→341 (389)	315→390 (438)
29→47 (95)	70→96 (144)	111→146 (194)	152→195 (243)	193→244 (292)	234→293 (341)	275→342 (390)	316→392 (440)
30→48 (96)	71→98 (146)	112→147 (195)	153→196 (244)	194→245 (293)	235→294 (342)	276→344 (392)	317→393 (441)
31→50 (98)	72→99 (147)	113→148 (196)	154→197 (245)	195→246 (294)	236→296 (344)	277→345 (393)	318→394 (442)
32→51 (99)	73→100 (148)	114→149 (197)	155→198 (246)	196→248 (296)	237→297 (345)	278→346 (394)	319→395 (443)
33→52 (100)	74→101 (149)	115→150 (198)	156→200 (248)	197→249 (297)	238→298 (346)	279→347 (395)	320→396 (444)
34→53 (101)	75→102 (150)	116→152 (200)	157→201 (249)	198→250 (298)	239→299 (347)	280→348 (396)	321→398 (446)
35→54 (102)	76→104 (152)	117→153 (201)	158→202 (250)	199→251 (299)	240→300 (348)	281→350 (398)	322→399 (447)
36→56 (104)	77→105 (153)	118→154 (202)	159→203 (251)	200→252 (300)	241→302 (350)	282→351 (399)	323→400 (448)
37→57 (105)	78→106 (154)	119→155 (203)	160→204 (252)	201→254 (302)	242→303 (351)	283→352 (400)	324→401 (449)
38→58 (106)	79→107 (155)	120→156 (204)	161→206 (254)	202→255 (303)	243→304 (352)	284→353 (401)	325→402 (450)
39→59 (107)	80→108 (156)	121→158 (206)	162→207 (255)	203→256 (304)	244→305 (353)	285→354 (402)	326→404 (452)
40→60 (108)	81→110 (158)	122→159 (207)	163→208 (256)	204→257 (305)	245→306 (354)	286→356 (404)	327→405 (453)
41→62 (110)	82→111 (159)	123→160 (208)	164→209 (257)	205→258 (306)	246→308 (356)	287→357 (405)	328→406 (454)
42→63 (111)	83→112 (160)	124→161 (209)	165→210 (258)	206→260 (308)	247→309 (357)	288→358 (406)	329→407 (455)
43→64 (112)	84→113 (161)	125→162 (210)	166→212 (260)	207→261 (309)	248→310 (358)	289→359 (407)	330→408 (456)
44→65 (113)	85→114 (162)	126→164 (212)	167→213 (261)	208→262 (310)	249→311 (359)	290→360 (408)	331→410 (458)
45→66 (114)	86→115 (164)	127→165 (213)	168→214 (262)	209→263 (311)	250→312 (360)	291→362 (410)	332→411 (459)
46→68 (116)	87→117 (165)	128→166 (214)	169→215 (263)	210→264 (312)	251→314 (362)	292→363 (411)	333→412 (460)
47→69 (117)	88→118 (166)	129→167 (215)	170→216 (264)	211→266 (314)	252→315 (363)	293→364 (412)	334→413 (461)
48→70 (118)	89→119 (167)	130→168 (216)	171→218 (266)	212→267 (315)	253→316 (364)	294→365 (413)	335→414 (462)
49→71 (119)	90→120 (168)	131→170 (218)	172→219 (267)	213→268 (316)	254→317 (365)	295→366 (414)	336→416 (464)
50→72 (120)	91→122 (170)	132→171 (219)	173→220 (268)	214→269 (317)	255→318 (366)	296→368 (416)	337→417 (465)
51→74 (122)	92→123 (171)	133→172 (220)	174→221 (269)	215→270 (318)	256→320 (368)	297→369 (417)	338→418 (466)
52→75 (123)	93→124 (172)	134→173 (221)	175→222 (270)	216→271 (320)	257→321 (369)	298→370 (418)	339→419 (467)
53→76 (124)	94→125 (173)	135→174 (222)	176→224 (272)	217→273 (321)	258→322 (370)	299→371 (419)	
54→77 (125)	95→126 (174)	136→176 (224)	177→225 (273)	218→274 (322)	259→323 (371)	300→372 (420)	
55→78 (126)	96→128 (176)	137→177 (225)	178→226 (274)	219→275 (323)	260→324 (372)	301→374 (422)	

FOR OFFENSE CLASSES F THROUGH I [Minimum Sentence → Corresponding Maximum]

3→13	9→20	15→27	21→35	27→42	33→49	39→56	45→63
4→14	10→21	16→29	22→36	28→43	34→50	40→57	46→65
5→15	11→23	17→30	23→37	29→44	35→51	41→59	47→66
6→17	12→24	18→31	24→38	30→45	36→53	42→60	48→67
7→18	13→25	19→32	25→39	31→47	37→54	43→61	49→68
8→19	14→26	20→33	26→41	32→48	38→55	44→62	

Length of Probation Period

The original period of probation for a felony sentenced under Structured Sentencing must fall within the following limits:

- Community—12 to 30 months
- Intermediate—18 to 36 months

The court may depart from those ranges with a finding that a longer or shorter period is required. The maximum permissible period with a finding is 5 years. G.S. 15A-1343.2.

Post-Release Supervision

Class F–I felony—9 months
Class B1–E felony—12 months
Crimes requiring sex offender registration—5 years

Fines

Any felony sentence may include a fine. Unless otherwise provided for a specific offense, the amount of the fine is in the discretion of the court. G.S. 15A-1340.17(b).

Felony Offenses Committed **December 1, 2009**, through **November 30, 2011**
MINIMUM SENTENCES AND DISPOSITIONAL OPTIONS

OFFENSE CLASS	PRIOR RECORD LEVEL						DISPOSITION
	I 0–1 Pt	II 2–5 Pts	III 6–9 Pts	IV 10–13 Pts	V 14–17 Pts	VI 18+ Pts	
A Max. Death or Life w/o Parole	Death or Life without Parole — Defendant under 18 at Time of Offense: Life with or without Parole						
B1 Max. Life w/o Parole	A 240–300 / **192–240** / 144–192	A 276–345 / **221–276** / 166–221	A 317–397 / **254–317** / 190–254	A 365–456 / **292–365** / 219–292	A Life w/o Parole / **336–420** / 252–336	A Life w/o Parole / **386–483** / 290–386	Aggravated / **PRESUMPTIVE** / Mitigated
B2 Max. 481	A EM 157–196 / **125–157** / 94–125	A EM 180–225 / **144–180** / 108–144	A 207–258 / **165–207** / 124–165	A 238–297 / **190–238** / 143–190	A 273–342 / **219–273** / 164–219	A 314–393 / **251–314** / 189–251	
C Max. 228	A EM 73–92 / **58–73** / 44–58	A EM 83–104 / **67–83** / 50–67	A 96–120 / **77–96** / 58–77	A 110–138 / **88–110** / 66–88	A 127–159 / **101–127** / 76–101	A 146–182 / **117–146** / 87–117	
D Max. 201	A EM 64–80 / **51–64** / ASR 38–51	A EM 73–92 / **59–73** / ASR 44–59	A 84–105 / **67–84** / ASR 51–67	A 97–121 / **78–97** / 58–78	A 111–139 / **89–111** / 67–89	A 128–160 / **103–128** / 77–103	
E Max. 85	I/A 25–31 / **20–25** / ASR 15–20	I/A 29–36 / **23–29** / ASR 17–23	A 33–41 / **26–33** / ASR 20–26	A 38–48 / **30–38** / ASR 23–30	A 44–55 / **35–44** / 26–35	A 50–63 / **40–50** / 30–40	
F Max. 50	I/A 16–20 / **13–16** / ASR 10–13	I/A 19–23 / **15–19** / ASR 11–15	I/A 21–27 / **17–21** / ASR 13–17	A 25–31 / **20–25** / ASR 15–20	A 28–36 / **23–28** / ASR 17–23	A 33–41 / **26–33** / 20–26	
G Max. 38	I/A 13–16 / **10–13** / ASR 8–10	I/A 14–18 / **12–14** / ASR 9–12	I/A 17–21 / **13–17** / ASR 10–13	I/A 19–24 / **15–19** / ASR 11–15	A 22–27 / **17–22** / ASR 13–17	A 25–31 / **20–25** / ASR 15–20	
H Max. 30	C/I/A 6–8 / **5–6** / ASR 4–5	I/A 8–10 / **6–8** / ASR 4–6	I/A 10–12 / **8–10** / 6–8	I/A 11–14 / **9–11** / ASR 7–9	I/A 15–19 / **12–15** / ASR 9–12	A 20–25 / **16–20** / ASR 12–16	
I Max. 15	C 6–8 / **4–6** / 3–4	C/I 6–8 / **4–6** / 3–4	I 6–8 / **5–6** / 4–5	I/A 8–10 / **6–8** / 4–6	I/A 9–11 / **7–9** / 5–7	I/A 10–12 / **8–10** / 6–8	

Note: Numbers shown are in months. The number shown below each offense class reflects the maximum possible sentence for that class of offense (the highest maximum sentence from the aggravated range in prior record level VI).

A—Active Punishment
I—Intermediate Punishment
C—Community Punishment

EM Extraordinary Mitigation (possible eligibility). *See page 10.*

ASR Advanced Supervised Release (possible eligibility). *See page 10.*

MAXIMUM SENTENCES

The tables below show the maximum sentence that corresponds to each minimum sentence. For minimum sentences of 340 months or more, the maximum sentence is 120 percent of the minimum sentence, rounded to the next highest month, plus 9 additional months. G.S. 15A-1340.17(e1).

FOR OFFENSE CLASSES B1 THROUGH E [Minimum Sentence → Corresponding Maximum]

15→27	56→77	97→126	138→175	179→224	220→273	261→323	302→372
16→29	57→78	98→127	139→176	180→225	221→275	262→324	303→373
17→30	58→79	99→128	140→177	181→227	222→276	263→325	304→374
18→31	59→80	100→129	141→179	182→228	223→277	264→326	305→375
19→32	60→81	101→131	142→180	183→229	224→278	265→327	306→377
20→33	61→83	102→132	143→181	184→230	225→279	266→329	307→378
21→35	62→84	103→133	144→182	185→231	226→281	267→330	308→379
22→36	63→85	104→134	145→183	186→233	227→282	268→331	309→380
23→37	64→86	105→135	146→185	187→234	228→283	269→332	310→381
24→38	65→87	106→137	147→186	188→235	229→284	270→333	311→383
25→39	66→89	107→138	148→187	189→236	230→285	271→335	312→384
26→41	67→90	108→139	149→188	190→237	231→287	272→336	313→385
27→42	68→91	109→140	150→189	191→239	232→288	273→337	314→386
28→43	69→92	110→141	151→191	192→240	233→289	274→338	315→387
29→44	70→93	111→143	152→192	193→241	234→290	275→339	316→389
30→45	71→95	112→144	153→193	194→242	235→291	276→341	317→390
31→47	72→96	113→145	154→194	195→243	236→293	277→342	318→391
32→48	73→97	114→146	155→195	196→245	237→294	278→343	319→392
33→49	74→98	115→147	156→197	197→246	238→295	279→344	320→393
34→50	75→99	116→149	157→198	198→247	239→296	280→345	321→395
35→51	76→101	117→150	158→199	199→248	240→297	281→347	322→396
36→53	77→102	118→151	159→200	200→249	241→299	282→348	323→397
37→54	78→103	119→152	160→201	201→251	242→300	283→349	324→398
38→55	79→104	120→153	161→203	202→252	243→301	284→350	325→399
39→56	80→105	121→155	162→204	203→253	244→302	285→351	326→401
40→57	81→107	122→156	163→205	204→254	245→303	286→353	327→402
41→59	82→108	123→157	164→206	205→255	246→305	287→354	328→403
42→60	83→109	124→158	165→207	206→257	247→306	288→355	329→404
43→61	84→110	125→159	166→209	207→258	248→307	289→356	330→405
44→62	85→111	126→161	167→210	208→259	249→308	290→357	331→407
45→63	86→113	127→162	168→211	209→260	250→309	291→359	332→408
46→65	87→114	128→163	169→212	210→261	251→311	292→360	333→409
47→66	88→115	129→164	170→213	211→263	252→312	293→361	334→410
48→67	89→116	130→165	171→215	212→264	253→313	294→362	335→411
49→68	90→117	131→167	172→216	213→265	254→314	295→363	336→413
50→69	91→119	132→168	173→217	214→266	255→315	296→365	337→414
51→71	92→120	133→169	174→218	215→267	256→317	297→366	338→415
52→72	93→121	134→170	175→219	216→269	257→318	298→367	339→416
53→73	94→122	135→171	176→221	217→270	258→319	299→368	
54→74	95→123	136→173	177→222	218→271	259→320	300→369	
55→75	96→125	137→174	178→223	219→272	260→321	301→371	

FOR OFFENSE CLASSES F THROUGH I [Minimum Sentence → Corresponding Maximum]

3→4	9→11	15→18	21→26	27→33	33→40	39→47	45→54
4→5	10→12	16→20	22→27	28→34	34→41	40→48	46→56
5→6	11→14	17→21	23→28	29→35	35→42	41→50	47→57
6→8	12→15	18→22	24→29	30→36	36→44	42→51	48→58
7→9	13→16	19→23	25→30	31→38	37→45	43→52	49→59
8→10	14→17	20→24	26→32	32→39	38→46	44→53	

Length of Probation Period

The original period of probation for a felony sentenced under Structured Sentencing must fall within the following limits:

- Community—12 to 30 months
- Intermediate—18 to 36 months

The court may depart from those ranges with a finding that a longer or shorter period is required. The maximum permissible period with a finding is 5 years. G.S. 15A-1343.2.

Post-Release Supervision

Class F–I felony—none
Class B1–E felony—9 months
Crimes requiring sex offender registration—5 years

Fines

Any felony sentence may include a fine. Unless otherwise provided for a specific offense, the amount of the fine is in the discretion of the court. G.S. 15A-1340.17(b).

Felony Offenses Committed December 1, 1995, through November 30, 2009
MINIMUM SENTENCES AND DISPOSITIONAL OPTIONS

OFFENSE CLASS	PRIOR RECORD LEVEL						DISPOSITION
	I 0 Pts	II 1–4 Pts	III 5–8 Pts	IV 9–14 Pts	V 15–18 Pts	VI 19+ Pts	
A Max. Death or Life w/o Parole	Death or Life without Parole — Defendant under 18 at Time of Offense: Life with or without Parole						
B1 Max. Life w/o Parole	A 240–300 **192–240** 144–192	A 288–360 **230–288** 173–230	A 336–420 **269–336** 202–269	A 384–480 **307–384** 230–307	A Life w/o Parole **346–433** 260–346	A Life w/o Parole **384–480** 288–384	Aggravated **PRESUMPTIVE** Mitigated
B2 Max. 480	A ᴱᴹ 157–196 **125–157** 94–125	A ᴱᴹ 189–237 **151–189** 114–151	A 220–276 **176–220** 132–176	A 251–313 **201–251** 151–201	A 282–353 **225–282** 169–225	A 313–392 **251–313** 188–251	
C Max. 261	A ᴱᴹ 73–92 **58–73** 44–58	A ᴱᴹ 100–125 **80–100** 60–80	A 116–145 **93–116** 70–93	A 133–167 **107–133** 80–107	A 151–188 **121–151** 90–121	A 168–210 **135–168** 101–135	
D Max. 229	A ᴱᴹ 64–80 **51–64** ASR 38–51	A ᴱᴹ 77–95 **61–77** ASR 46–61	A 103–129 **82–103** ASR 61–82	A 117–146 **94–117** 71–94	A 133–167 **107–133** 80–107	A 146–183 **117–146** 88–117	
E Max. 98	I/A 25–31 **20–25** ASR 15–20	I/A 29–36 **23–29** ASR 17–23	A 34–42 **27–34** ASR 20–27	A 46–58 **37–46** ASR 28–37	A 53–66 **42–53** 32–42	A 59–74 **47–59** 35–47	
F Max. 59	I/A 16–20 **13–16** ASR 10–13	I/A 19–24 **15–19** ASR 11–15	I/A 21–26 **17–21** ASR 13–17	A 25–31 **20–25** ASR 15–20	A 34–42 **27–34** 20–27	A 39–49 **31–39** 23–31	
G Max. 44	I/A 13–16 **10–13** ASR 8–10	I/A 15–19 **12–15** ASR 9–12	I/A 16–20 **13–16** ASR 10–13	I/A 20–25 **16–20** ASR 12–16	A 21–26 **17–21** ASR 13–17	A 29–36 **23–29** ASR 17–23	
H Max. 30	C/I/A 6–8 **5–6** ASR 4–5	I/A 8–10 **6–8** ASR 4–6	I/A 10–12 **8–10** ASR 6–8	I/A 11–14 **9–11** ASR 7–9	I/A 15–19 **12–15** ASR 9–12	A 20–25 **16–20** ASR 12–16	
I Max. 15	C 6–8 **4–6** 3–4	C/I 6–8 **4–6** 3–4	I 6–8 **5–6** 4–5	I/A 8–10 **6–8** 4–6	I/A 9–11 **7–9** 5–7	I/A 10–12 **8–10** 6–8	

Note: Numbers shown are in months. The number shown below each offense class reflects the maximum possible sentence for that class of offense (the highest maximum sentence from the aggravated range in prior record level VI).

A—Active Punishment
I—Intermediate Punishment
C—Community Punishment

ᴱᴹ **Extraordinary Mitigation** (possible eligibility). *See* page 10.

ASR **Advanced Supervised Release** (possible eligibility). *See* page 10.

40

MAXIMUM SENTENCES

The tables below show the maximum sentence that corresponds to each minimum sentence. For minimum sentences of 340 months or more, the maximum sentence is 120 percent of the minimum sentence, rounded to the next highest month, plus 9 additional months. G.S. 15A-1340.17(e1).

FOR OFFENSE CLASSES B1 THROUGH E [Minimum Sentence → Corresponding Maximum]

15→27	56→77	97→126	138→175	179→224	220→273	261→323	302→372
16→29	57→78	98→127	139→176	180→225	221→275	262→324	303→373
17→30	58→79	99→128	140→177	181→227	222→276	263→325	304→374
18→31	59→80	100→129	141→179	182→228	223→277	264→326	305→375
19→32	60→81	101→131	142→180	183→229	224→278	265→327	306→377
20→33	61→83	102→132	143→181	184→230	225→279	266→329	307→378
21→35	62→84	103→133	144→182	185→231	226→281	267→330	308→379
22→36	63→85	104→134	145→183	186→233	227→282	268→331	309→380
23→37	64→86	105→135	146→185	187→234	228→283	269→332	310→381
24→38	65→87	106→137	147→186	188→235	229→284	270→333	311→383
25→39	66→89	107→138	148→187	189→236	230→285	271→335	312→384
26→41	67→90	108→139	149→188	190→237	231→287	272→336	313→385
27→42	68→91	109→140	150→189	191→239	232→288	273→337	314→386
28→43	69→92	110→141	151→191	192→240	233→289	274→338	315→387
29→44	70→93	111→143	152→192	193→241	234→290	275→339	316→389
30→45	71→95	112→144	153→193	194→242	235→291	276→341	317→390
31→47	72→96	113→145	154→194	195→243	236→293	277→342	318→391
32→48	73→97	114→146	155→195	196→245	237→294	278→343	319→392
33→49	74→98	115→147	156→197	197→246	238→295	279→344	320→393
34→50	75→99	116→149	157→198	198→247	239→296	280→345	321→395
35→51	76→101	117→150	158→199	199→248	240→297	281→347	322→396
36→53	77→102	118→151	159→200	200→249	241→299	282→348	323→397
37→54	78→103	119→152	160→201	201→251	242→300	283→349	324→398
38→55	79→104	120→153	161→203	202→252	243→301	284→350	325→399
39→56	80→105	121→155	162→204	203→253	244→302	285→351	326→401
40→57	81→107	122→156	163→205	204→254	245→303	286→353	327→402
41→59	82→108	123→157	164→206	205→255	246→305	287→354	328→403
42→60	83→109	124→158	165→207	206→257	247→306	288→355	329→404
43→61	84→110	125→159	166→209	207→258	248→307	289→356	330→405
44→62	85→111	126→161	167→210	208→259	249→308	290→357	331→407
45→63	86→113	127→162	168→211	209→260	250→309	291→359	332→408
46→65	87→114	128→163	169→212	210→261	251→311	292→360	333→409
47→66	88→115	129→164	170→213	211→263	252→312	293→361	334→410
48→67	89→116	130→165	171→215	212→264	253→313	294→362	335→411
49→68	90→117	131→167	172→216	213→265	254→314	295→363	336→413
50→69	91→119	132→168	173→217	214→266	255→315	296→365	337→414
51→71	92→120	133→169	174→218	215→267	256→317	297→366	338→415
52→72	93→121	134→170	175→219	216→269	257→318	298→367	339→416
53→73	94→122	135→171	176→221	217→270	258→319	299→368	
54→74	95→123	136→173	177→222	218→271	259→320	300→369	
55→75	96→125	137→174	178→223	219→272	260→321	301→371	

FOR OFFENSE CLASSES F THROUGH I [Minimum Sentence → Corresponding Maximum]

3→4	9→11	15→18	21→26	27→33	33→40	39→47	45→54
4→5	10→12	16→20	22→27	28→34	34→41	40→48	46→56
5→6	11→14	17→21	23→28	29→35	35→42	41→50	47→57
6→8	12→15	18→22	24→29	30→36	36→44	42→51	48→58
7→9	13→16	19→23	25→30	31→38	37→45	43→52	49→59
8→10	14→17	20→24	26→32	32→39	38→46	44→53	

Length of Probation Period
The original period of probation for a felony sentenced under Structured Sentencing must fall within the following limits:

- Community—12 to 30 months
- Intermediate—18 to 36 months

The court may depart from those ranges with a finding that a longer or shorter period is required. The maximum permissible period with a finding is 5 years. G.S. 15A-1343.2.

Post-Release Supervision
Class F–I felony—none
Class B1–E felony—9 months
Crimes requiring sex offender registration (offenses committed on or after Dec. 1, 1996)—5 years

Fines
Any felony sentence may include a fine. Unless otherwise provided for a specific offense, the amount of the fine is in the discretion of the court. G.S. 15A-1340.17(b).

OFFENSE CLASS	PRIOR RECORD LEVEL						DISPOSITION
	I 0 Pts	**II** 1–4 Pts	**III** 5–8 Pts	**IV** 9–14 Pts	**V** 15–18 Pts	**VI** 19+ Pts	
A Max. Death or Life w/o Parole	Death or Life without Parole — Defendant under 18 at Time of Offense: Life with or without Parole						
B1 Max. Life w/o Parole	A 240–300 **192–240** 144–192	A 288–360 **230–288** 173–230	A 336–420 **269–336** 202–269	A 384–480 **307–384** 230–307	A Life w/o Parole **346–433** 260–346	A Life w/o Parole **384–480** 288–384	Aggravated **PRESUMPTIVE** Mitigated
B2 Max. 415	A ᴱᴹ 135–169 **108–135** 81–108	A ᴱᴹ 163–204 **130–163** 98–130	A 190–238 **152–190** 114–152	A 216–270 **173–216** 130–173	A 243–304 **194–243** 146–194	A 270–338 **216–270** 162–216	
C Max. 227	A ᴱᴹ 63–79 **50–63** 38–50	A ᴱᴹ 86–108 **69–86** 52–69	A 100–125 **80–100** 60–80	A 115–144 **92–115** 69–92	A 130–162 **104–130** 78–104	A 145–181 **116–145** 87–116	
D Max. 199	A ᴱᴹ 55–69 **44–55** ᴬˢᴿ 33–44	A ᴱᴹ 66–82 **53–66** ᴬˢᴿ 40–53	A 89–111 **71–89** ᴬˢᴿ 53–71	A 101–126 **81–101** 61–81	A 115–144 **92–115** 69–92	A 126–158 **101–126** 76–101	
E Max. 98	I/A 25–31 **20–25** ᴬˢᴿ 15–20	I/A 29–36 **23–39** ᴬˢᴿ 17–23	A 34–42 **27–34** ᴬˢᴿ 20–27	A 46–58 **37–46** ᴬˢᴿ 28–37	A 53–66 **42–53** 32–42	A 59–74 **47–59** 35–47	
F Max. 59	I/A 16–20 **13–16** ᴬˢᴿ 10–13	I/A 19–24 **15–19** ᴬˢᴿ 11–15	I/A 21–26 **17–21** 13–17	A 25–31 **20–25** ᴬˢᴿ 15–20	A 34–42 **27–34** ᴬˢᴿ 20–27	A 39–49 **31–39** 23–31	
G Max. 44	I/A 13–16 **10–13** ᴬˢᴿ 8–10	I/A 15–19 **12–15** ᴬˢᴿ 9–12	I/A 16–20 **13–16** ᴬˢᴿ 10–13	I/A 20–25 **16–20** ᴬˢᴿ 12–16	A 21–26 **17–21** ᴬˢᴿ 13–17	A 29–36 **23–29** ᴬˢᴿ 17–23	
H Max. 30	C/I 6–8 **5–6** ᴬˢᴿ 4–5	I 8–10 **6–8** ᴬˢᴿ 4–6	I/A 10–12 **8–10** ᴬˢᴿ 6–8	I/A 11–14 **9–11** ᴬˢᴿ 7–9	I/A 15–19 **12–15** ᴬˢᴿ 9–12	A 20–25 **16–20** ᴬˢᴿ 12–16	
I Max. 15	C 6–8 **4–6** 3–4	C/I 6–8 **4–6** 3–4	I 6–8 **5–6** 4–5	I/A 8–10 **6–8** 4–6	I/A 9–11 **7–9** 5–7	I/A 10–12 **8–10** 6–8	

Note: Numbers shown are in months. The number shown below each offense class reflects the maximum possible sentence for that class of offense (the highest maximum sentence from the aggravated range in prior record level VI).

A—Active Punishment
I—Intermediate Punishment
C—Community Punishment

ᴱᴹ **Extraordinary Mitigation** (possible eligibility). *See* page 10.

ᴬˢᴿ **Advanced Supervised Release** (possible eligibility). *See* page 10.

MAXIMUM SENTENCES

The tables below show the maximum sentence that corresponds to each minimum sentence. For minimum sentences of 340 months or more, the maximum sentence is 120 percent of the minimum sentence, rounded to the next highest month, plus 9 additional months. G.S. 15A-1340.17(e1).

FOR OFFENSE CLASSES B1 THROUGH E [Minimum Sentence → Corresponding Maximum]

15→27	58→79	101→131	144→182	187→234	230→285	273→337	316→389
16→29	59→80	102→132	145→183	188→235	231→287	274→338	317→390
17→30	60→81	103→133	146→185	189→236	232→288	275→339	318→391
18→31	61→83	104→134	147→186	190→237	233→289	276→341	319→392
19→32	62→84	105→135	148→187	191→239	234→290	277→342	320→393
20→33	63→85	106→137	149→188	192→240	235→291	278→343	321→395
21→35	64→86	107→138	150→189	193→241	236→293	279→344	322→396
22→36	65→87	108→139	151→191	194→242	237→294	280→345	323→397
23→37	66→89	109→140	152→192	195→243	238→295	281→347	324→398
24→38	67→90	110→141	153→193	196→245	239→296	282→348	325→399
25→39	68→91	111→143	154→194	197→246	240→297	283→349	326→401
26→41	69→92	112→144	155→195	198→247	241→299	284→350	327→402
27→42	70→93	113→145	156→197	199→248	242→300	285→351	328→403
28→43	71→95	114→146	157→198	200→249	243→301	286→353	329→404
29→44	72→96	115→147	158→199	201→251	244→302	287→354	330→405
30→45	73→97	116→149	159→200	202→252	245→303	288→355	331→407
31→47	74→98	117→150	160→201	203→253	246→305	289→356	332→408
32→48	75→99	118→151	161→203	204→254	247→306	290→357	333→409
33→49	76→101	119→152	162→204	205→255	248→307	291→359	334→410
34→50	77→102	120→153	163→205	206→257	249→308	292→360	335→411
35→51	78→103	121→155	164→206	207→258	250→309	293→361	336→413
36→53	79→104	122→156	165→207	208→259	251→311	294→362	337→414
37→54	80→105	123→157	166→209	209→260	252→312	295→363	338→415
38→55	81→107	124→158	167→210	210→261	253→313	296→365	339→416
39→56	82→108	125→159	168→211	211→263	254→314	297→366	
40→57	83→109	126→161	169→212	212→264	255→315	298→367	
41→59	84→110	127→162	170→213	213→265	256→317	299→368	
42→60	85→111	128→163	171→215	214→266	257→318	300→369	
43→61	86→113	129→164	172→216	215→267	258→319	301→371	
44→62	87→114	130→165	173→217	216→269	259→320	302→372	
45→63	88→115	131→167	174→218	217→270	260→321	303→373	
46→65	89→116	132→168	175→219	218→271	261→323	304→374	
47→66	90→117	133→169	176→221	219→272	262→324	305→375	
48→67	91→119	134→170	177→222	220→273	263→325	306→377	
49→68	92→120	135→171	178→223	221→275	264→326	307→378	
50→69	93→121	136→173	179→224	222→276	265→327	308→379	
51→71	94→122	137→174	180→225	223→277	266→329	309→380	
52→72	95→123	138→175	181→227	224→278	267→330	310→381	
53→73	96→125	139→176	182→228	225→279	268→331	311→383	
54→74	97→126	140→177	183→229	226→281	269→332	312→384	
55→75	98→127	141→179	184→230	227→282	270→333	313→385	
56→77	99→128	142→180	185→231	228→283	271→335	314→386	
57→78	100→129	143→181	186→233	229→284	272→336	315→387	

FOR OFFENSE CLASSES F THROUGH I [Minimum Sentence → Corresponding Maximum]

3→4	9→11	15→18	21→26	27→33	33→40	39→47	45→54
4→5	10→12	16→20	22→27	28→34	34→41	40→48	46→56
5→6	11→14	17→21	23→28	29→35	35→42	41→50	47→57
6→8	12→15	18→22	24→29	30→36	36→44	42→51	48→58
7→9	13→16	19→23	25→30	31→38	37→45	43→52	49→59
8→10	14→17	20→24	26→32	32→39	38→46	44→53	

Length of Probation Period

The original period of probation for a felony sentenced under Structured Sentencing must fall within the following limits:

- Community—12 to 30 months
- Intermediate—18 to 36 months

The court may depart from those ranges with a finding that a longer or shorter period is required. The maximum permissible period with a finding is 5 years. G.S. 15A-1343.2.

Post-Release Supervision

Class F–I felony—none
Class B1–E felony—6 months

Fines

Any felony sentence may include a fine. Unless otherwise provided for a specific offense, the amount of the fine is in the discretion of the court. G.S. 15A-1340.17(b).

Misdemeanor Offenses Committed on or after **December 1, 2013**

OFFENSE CLASS	PRIOR CONVICTION LEVEL			
	I No Prior Convictions	**II** One to Four Prior Convictions		**III** Five or More Prior Convictions
A1	**C/I/A** 1–60 days	**C/I/A** 1–75 days		**C/I/A** 1–150 days
1	**C** 1–45 days	**C/I/A** 1–45 days		**C/I/A** 1–120 days
2	**C** 1–30 days	**C/I** 1–45 days		**C/I/A** 1–60 days
		One to Three Prior Convictions	**Four Prior Convictions**	
3	**C** Fine Only* 1–10 days	**C** Fine Only* 1–15 days	**C/I** 1–15 days	**C/I/A** 1–20 days

*Unless otherwise provided for a specific offense, the judgment for a person convicted of a Class 3 misdemeanor who has no more than three prior convictions shall consist only of a fine.

A—Active Punishment   **I**—Intermediate Punishment   **C**—Community Punishment

Length of Probation Period

The original period of probation for a misdemeanor sentenced under Structured Sentencing must fall within the following limits:

- Community—6 to 18 months
- Intermediate—12 to 24 months

The court may depart from those ranges with a finding that a longer or shorter period is required. The maximum permissible period with a finding is 5 years. G.S. 15A-1343.2.

Fines

Any misdemeanor sentence may include a fine. Unless otherwise provided for a specific offense, the maximum fine for a misdemeanor is as follows:

- Class A1—Court discretion
- Class 1—Court discretion
- Class 2—$1,000
- Class 3—$200

Local ordinance violation: $50, unless the ordinance provides for a larger amount, up to $500. G.S. 15A-1340.23(b); 14-4.

Punishment for Covered Driving While Impaired (DWI) Offenses
Committed on or after **October 1, 2013**

Punishment Level Controlling Statute *Factors*	Imprisonment and Mandatory Probation Conditions	Fine

Aggravated Level One
G.S. 20-179(f3)
Three or more grossly aggravating factors
	• 12 months minimum to 36 months maximum
	• If suspended
	  – Imprisonment of at least 120 days as a condition of special probation
	  – Requirement that defendant abstain from alcohol consumption for a minimum of 120 days to a maximum of the term of probation, as verified by continuous alcohol monitoring (CAM) system
	  – Requirement that defendant obtain a substance abuse assessment and education or treatment required by G.S. 20-17.6
		Up to $10,000

Level One
G.S. 20-179(g)
Grossly aggravating factor in G.S. 20-179(c)(4) or two other grossly aggravating factors
	• 30 days minimum to 24 months maximum
	• If suspended
	  – Special probation requiring (1) imprisonment of at least 30 days or (2) imprisonment of at least 10 days and alcohol abstinence and CAM for at least 120 days
	  – Requirement that defendant obtain a substance abuse assessment and education or treatment required by G.S. 20-17.6
		Up to $4,000

Level Two
G.S. 20-179(h)
One grossly aggravating factor, other than the grossly aggravating factor in G.S. 20-179(c)(4)
	• 7 days minimum to 12 months maximum
	• If suspended
	  – Special probation requiring (1) imprisonment of at least 7 days or (2) alcohol abstinence and CAM for at least 90 days
	    ○ If Level Two based on prior conviction or DWLR for an impaired driving revocation and prior conviction occurred within five years, sentence must require 240 hours of community service if no imprisonment imposed
	  – Requirement that defendant obtain a substance abuse assessment and education or treatment required by G.S. 20-17.6
		Up to $2,000

Level Three
G.S. 20-179(i)
Aggravating factors substantially outweigh any mitigating factors
	• 72 hours minimum to 6 months maximum
	• If suspended
	  – Must require one or both of the following
	    ○ Imprisonment for at least 72 hours as a condition of special probation
	    ○ Community service for a term of at least 72 hours
	  – Requirement that defendant obtain a substance abuse assessment and education or treatment required by G.S. 20-17.6
		Up to $1,000

Level Four
G.S. 20-179(j)
No aggravating and mitigating factors or aggravating factors are substantially counterbalanced by mitigating factors
	• 48 hours minimum to 120 days maximum
	• If suspended
	  – Must require one or both of the following
	    ○ Imprisonment for 48 hours as a condition of special probation
	    ○ Community service for a term of 48 hours
	  – Requirement that defendant obtain a substance abuse assessment and education or treatment required by G.S. 20-17.6
		Up to $500

Level Five
G.S. 20-179(k)
Mitigating factors substantially outweigh aggravating factors
	• 24 hours minimum to 60 days maximum
	• If suspended
	  – Must require one or both of the following
	    ○ Imprisonment for 24 hours as a condition of special probation
	    ○ Community service for a term of 24 hours
	  – Requirement that defendant obtain a substance abuse assessment and education or treatment required by G.S. 20-17.6
		Up to $200

Punishment for Covered DWI Offenses
Committed on or after **December 1, 2012,** and before **October 1, 2013**

Punishment Level Controlling Statute *Factors*	Imprisonment and Mandatory Probation Conditions	Fine

Aggravated Level One
G.S. 20-179(f3)
Three or more grossly aggravating factors
	• 12 months minimum to 36 months maximum
	• If suspended
	  – Imprisonment of at least 120 days as a condition of special probation
	  – Requirement that defendant abstain from alcohol consumption for a minimum of 120 days to a maximum of the term of probation, as verified by continuous alcohol monitoring (CAM) system
	  – Requirement that defendant obtain a substance abuse assessment and education or treatment required by G.S. 20-17.6
		Up to $10,000

Level One
G.S. 20-179(g)
Grossly aggravating factor in G.S. 20-179(c)(4) or two other grossly aggravating factors
	• 30 days minimum to 24 months maximum
	• If suspended
	  – Special probation requiring (1) imprisonment of at least 30 days or (2) imprisonment of at least 10 days and alcohol abstinence and CAM for at least 120 days
	  – Requirement that defendant obtain a substance abuse assessment and education or treatment required by G.S. 20-17.6
		Up to $4,000

Level Two
G.S. 20-179(h)
One grossly aggravating factor, other than the grossly aggravating factor in G.S. 20-179(c)(4)
	• 7 days minimum to 12 months maximum
	• If suspended
	  – Special probation requiring (1) imprisonment of at least 7 days or (2) alcohol abstinence and CAM for at least 90 days
	  – Requirement that defendant obtain a substance abuse assessment and education or treatment required by G.S. 20-17.6
		Up to $2,000

Level Three
G.S. 20-179(i)
Aggravating factors substantially outweigh any mitigating factors
	• 72 hours minimum to 6 months maximum
	• If suspended
	  – Must require one or both of the following
	    ○ Imprisonment for at least 72 hours as a condition of special probation
	    ○ Community service for a term of at least 72 hours
	  – Requirement that defendant obtain a substance abuse assessment and education or treatment required by G.S. 20-17.6
		Up to $1,000

Level Four
G.S. 20-179(j)
No aggravating and mitigating factors or aggravating factors are substantially counterbalanced by mitigating factors
	• 48 hours minimum to 120 days maximum
	• If suspended
	  – Must require one or both of the following
	    ○ Imprisonment for 48 hours as a condition of special probation
	    ○ Community service for a term of 48 hours
	  – Requirement that defendant obtain a substance abuse assessment and education or treatment required by G.S. 20-17.6
		Up to $500

Level Five
G.S. 20-179(k)
Mitigating factors substantially outweigh aggravating factors
	• 24 hours minimum to 60 days maximum
	• If suspended
	  – Must require one or both of the following
	    ○ Imprisonment for 24 hours as a condition of special probation
	    ○ Community service for a term of 24 hours
	  – Requirement that defendant obtain a substance abuse assessment and education or treatment required by G.S. 20-17.6
		Up to $200

Punishment for Covered DWI Offenses
Committed on or after **December 1, 2011,** and before **December 1, 2012**

Punishment Level Controlling Statute *Factors*	Imprisonment and Mandatory Probation Conditions	Fine

Aggravated Level One
G.S. 20-179(f3)
Three or more grossly aggravating factors
	• 12 months minimum to 36 months maximum
	• If suspended
	  – Imprisonment of at least 120 days as a condition of special probation
	  – Requirement that defendant abstain from alcohol consumption for a minimum of 120 days to a maximum of the term of probation as verified by continuous alcohol monitoring (CAM) system
	  – Requirement that defendant obtain a substance abuse assessment and education or treatment required by G.S. 20-17.6
		Up to $10,000

Level One
G.S. 20-179(g)
Grossly aggravating factor in G.S. 20-179(c)(4) or two other grossly aggravating factors
	• 30 days minimum to 24 months maximum
	• If suspended
	  – Imprisonment of at least 30 days as a condition of special probation
	  – Requirement that defendant obtain a substance abuse assessment and education or treatment required by G.S. 20-17.6
		Up to $4,000

Level Two
G.S. 20-179(h)
One grossly aggravating factor, other than the grossly aggravating factor in G.S. 20-179(c)(4)
	• 7 days minimum to 12 months maximum
	• If suspended
	  – Imprisonment of at least 7 days as a condition of special probation
	  – Requirement that defendant obtain a substance abuse assessment and education or treatment required by G.S. 20-17.6
		Up to $2,000

Level Three
G.S. 20-179(i)
Aggravating factors substantially outweigh any mitigating factors
	• 72 hours minimum to 6 months maximum
	• If suspended
	  – Must require one or both of the following
	    ○ Imprisonment for at least 72 hours as a condition of special probation
	    ○ Community service for a term of at least 72 hours
	  – Requirement that defendant obtain a substance abuse assessment and education or treatment required by G.S. 20-17.6
		Up to $1,000

Level Four
G.S. 20-179(j)
No aggravating and mitigating factors or aggravating factors are substantially counterbalanced by mitigating factors
	• 48 hours minimum to 120 days maximum
	• If suspended
	  – Must require one or both of the following
	    ○ Imprisonment for 48 hours as a condition of special probation
	    ○ Community service for a term of 48 hours
	  – Requirement that defendant obtain a substance abuse assessment and education or treatment required by G.S. 20-17.6
		Up to $500

Level Five
G.S. 20-179(k)
Mitigating factors substantially outweigh aggravating factors
	• 24 hours minimum to 60 days maximum
	• If suspended
	  – Must require one or both of the following
	    ○ Imprisonment for 24 hours as a condition of special probation
	    ○ Community service for a term of 24 hours
	  – Requirement that defendant obtain a substance abuse assessment and education or treatment required by G.S. 20-17.6
		Up to $200

Punishment for Covered DWI Offenses
Committed on or after **December 1, 2007,** and before **December 1, 2011**

Punishment Level Controlling Statute *Factors*	**Imprisonment and Mandatory Probation Conditions**	**Fine**

Level One G.S. 20-179(g) *Two or more grossly aggravating factors*	• 30 days minimum to 24 months maximum
	• If suspended
	  – Imprisonment of at least 30 days as a condition of special probation
	  – Requirement that defendant obtain a substance abuse assessment and education or treatment required by G.S. 20-17.6
	  – Defendant may be required to abstain from alcohol for a minimum of 30 days up to a maximum of 60 days, as verified by a continuous alcohol monitoring (CAM) system
	    ○ Total cost of CAM may not exceed $1,000
		Up to $4,000

Level Two G.S. 20-179(h) *One grossly aggravating factor*	• 7 days minimum to 12 months maximum
	• If suspended
	  – Imprisonment of at least 7 days as a condition of special probation
	  – Requirement that defendant obtain a substance abuse assessment and education or treatment required by G.S. 20-17.6
	  – Defendant may be required to abstain from alcohol for a minimum of 30 days up to a maximum of 60 days, as verified by a CAM system
	    ○ Total cost of CAM may not exceed $1,000
		Up to $2,000

Level Three G.S. 20-179(i) *Aggravating factors substantially outweigh any mitigating factors*	• 72 hours minimum to 6 months maximum
	• If suspended
	  – Must require one or both of the following
	    ○ Imprisonment for at least 72 hours as a condition of special probation
	    ○ Community service for a term of at least 72 hours
	  – Requirement that defendant obtain a substance abuse assessment and education or treatment required by G.S. 20-17.6
		Up to $1,000

Level Four G.S. 20-179(j) *No aggravating and mitigating factors or aggravating factors are substantially counterbalanced by mitigating factors*	• 48 hours minimum to 120 days maximum
	• If suspended
	  – Must require one or both of the following
	    ○ Imprisonment for 48 hours as a condition of special probation
	    ○ Community service for a term of 48 hours
	  – Requirement that defendant obtain a substance abuse assessment and education or treatment required by G.S. 20-17.6
		Up to $500

Level Five G.S. 20-179(k) *Mitigating factors substantially outweigh aggravating factors*	• 24 hours minimum to 60 days maximum
	• If suspended
	  – Must require one or both of the following
	    ○ Imprisonment for 24 hours as a condition of special probation
	    ○ Community service for a term of 24 hours
	  – Requirement that defendant obtain a substance abuse assessment and education or treatment required by G.S. 20-17.6
		Up to $200

Drug Trafficking Sentencing (G.S. 90-95(h))

Drug trafficking is not sentenced using the regular Structured Sentencing grid. Instead, a person convicted of drug trafficking must be sentenced as set out below, including the mandatory fine, regardless of his or her prior criminal record.

Offense Class and Minimum Fines for Drug Trafficking

Drug	Amount	Class	Fine (not less than)
Marijuana	In excess of 10 lbs.–49 lbs.	H	$ 5,000
	50–1,999 lbs.	G	$ 25,000
	2,000–9,999	F	$ 50,000
	10,000 or more	D	$200,000
Methaqualone	1,000–4,999 dosage units	G	$ 25,000
	5,000–9,999	F	$ 50,000
	10,000 or more	D	$200,000
Cocaine	28–199 grams	G	$ 50,000
	200–399	F	$100,000
	400 or more	D	$250,000
Methamphetamine	28–199 grams	F	$ 50,000
	200–399	E	$100,000
	400 or more	C	$250,000
Amphetamine	28–199 grams	H	$ 5,000
	200–399	G	$ 25,000
	400 or more	E	$100,000
Opium, Opiate, Opioid, or Heroin*	4–13 grams	F	$ 50,000
	14–27	E	$100,000
	28 or more	C	$500,000
LSD	100–499 units	G	$ 25,000
	500–999	F	$ 50,000
	1,000 or more	D	$200,000
MDA/MDMA	100–499 units/28–199 grams	G	$ 25,000
	500–999 units/200–399 grams	F	$ 50,000
	1,000 units/400 grams or more	D	$250,000
Substituted Cathinones*	28–199 grams	F	$ 50,000
	200–399	E	$100,000
	400 or more	C	$250,000
Synthetic Cannabinoids	In excess of 50–249 dosage units**	H	$ 5,000
	250–1,249	G	$ 25,000
	1,250–3,749	F	$ 50,000
	3,750 or more	D	$200,000

* Effective December 1, 2018. S.L. 2018-44.

**A "dosage unit" is 3 grams of synthetic cannabinoid or any mixture containing such substance.

Minimum-Maximum Sentences for Drug Trafficking Crimes, by Offense Class

Class	Offense Committed **On/After** 12/1/2012		Offense Committed **Before** 12/1/2012	
	Minimum	Maximum	Minimum	Maximum
Class C	225 mos.	282	225 mos.	279
Class D	175	222	175	219
Class E	90	120	90	117
Class F	70	93	70	84
Class G	35	51	35	42
Class H	25	39	25	30

Consecutive Sentences

Trafficking sentences must run consecutively with any other sentence being served by the defendant. G.S. 90-95(h)(6). However, when a trafficking offense is disposed of in the same proceeding as another conviction, the court may impose concurrent or consolidated sentences. State v. Walston, 193 N.C. App. 134, 141–42 (2008).

Conspiracy to Commit Trafficking

Conspiracies to commit trafficking offenses are punishable the same as the target offense. G.S. 90-95(i).

Attempted Trafficking

Attempts to commit trafficking are the same **offense class** as the completed offense, but they are sentenced under the ordinary Structured Sentencing grid for that class of offense and prior record level, not the special mandatory sentences for completed trafficking offenses. G.S. 90-98.

Substantial Assistance

The judge sentencing a defendant for trafficking *may* reduce the fine, impose a prison term less than the applicable minimum, or suspend the prison term and place the defendant on probation when the defendant has provided substantial assistance in the identification, arrest, or conviction of any accomplices, accessories, co-conspirators, or principals. The sentencing judge must enter in the record a finding that the defendant has rendered such substantial assistance. G.S. 90-95(h)(5). The assistance offered need not be limited to accomplices, etc., involved in the defendant's individual case; the court is permitted to consider the defendant's assistance in the prosecution of other cases. State v. Baldwin, 66 N.C. App. 156, 158 (1984). The determination of whether or not the defendant has provided substantial assistance is within the discretion of the trial court. State v. Hamad, 92 N.C. App. 282, 289 (1988). Even when the court finds substantial assistance, the decision to reduce the defendant's sentence is in the court's discretion. State v. Wells, 104 N.C. App. 274, 276–77 (1991).

When substantial assistance applies, the court may select a minimum sentence of its choosing; it is not bound by the regular sentencing grid. State v. Saunders, 131 N.C. App. 551, 553 (1998). The court should order the maximum sentence that corresponds to the selected minimum sentence, based on the defendant's offense class and offense date.

Appendix A: Offense Class Table for Felonies

Class A

First-Degree Murder (G.S. 14-17)	

Class B1

Second-Degree Murder (G.S. 14-17)	Class B2 for offenses before 12/1/2012 and as provided below
First-Degree Forcible Rape (G.S. 14-27.21)	Was G.S. 14-27.2(a)(2) before 12/1/2015
First-Degree Forcible Sexual Offense (G.S.14-27.26)	Was G.S. 14-27.4(a)(2) before 12/1/2015
First-Degree Statutory Rape (G.S. 14-27.24)	Was G.S. 14-27.2(a)(1) before 12/1/2015
First-Degree Statutory Sexual Offense (G.S. 14-27.29)	Was G.S. 14-27.4(a)(1) before 12/1/2015
*Statutory Rape of a Child by an Adult (G.S. 14-27.23)	Was G.S. 14-27.2A before 12/1/2015
Statutory Rape of Person ≤ 15/Defendant 6+ Years Older (G.S. 14-27.25(a))	Was G.S. 14-27.7A(a) before 12/1/2015
*Statutory Sexual Offense with a Child by an Adult (G.S. 14-27.28)	Was G.S. 14-27.4A before 12/1/2015
Statutory Sexual Offense with Person ≤ 15/Defendant 6+ Years Older (G.S. 14-27.30(a))	Was G.S. 14-27.7A(a) before 12/1/2015

Class B2

Second-Degree Murder (G.S. 14-17(b)(1)–(2))	
Child Abuse, Serious Bodily Injury (G.S. 14-318.4(a3))	Class C for offenses before 12/1/2013

Class C

Assault with Deadly Weapon with Intent to Kill Inflicting Serious Injury (G.S. 14-32(a))	
Embezzlement, $100,000 or more (G.S. 14-90)	
First-Degree Kidnapping (G.S. 14-39)	
First-Degree Sexual Exploitation of a Minor (G.S. 14-190.16)	Class D for offenses before 12/1/2008
Larceny by Employee, $100,000 or More (G.S. 14-74)	
Manufacture of Methamphetamine (G.S. 90-95(b)(1a))	
Second-Degree Forcible Rape (G.S. 14-27.22)	Was G.S. 14-27.3 before 12/1/2015
Second-Degree Forcible Sexual Offense (G.S. 14-27.27)	Was G.S. 14-27.5 before 12/1/2015
Statutory Rape of Person ≤ 15/Defendant > 4, < 6 Years Older (G.S. 14-27.25(b))	Was G.S. 14-27.7A(b) before 12/1/2015
Statutory Sexual Offense with Person ≤ 15/Defendant > 4, < 6 Years Older (G.S. 14-27.30(b))	Was G.S. 14-27.7A(b) before 12/1/2015

Class D

*Aggravated Felony Death by Vehicle (G.S. 20-141.5(a5))	
Robbery with a Firearm or Dangerous Weapon (G.S. 14-87)	
Child Abuse, Serious Physical Injury or Sexual Act (G.S. 14-318.4(a) or (a2))	Class E for offenses before 12/1/2013
*Death by Vehicle (G.S. 20-141.4(a1))	Class G for offenses before 12/1/2006; Class E for offenses before 12/1/2012
Discharge Firearm into Occupied Dwelling or Vehicle in Operation (G.S. 14-34.1)	
First-Degree Arson (G.S. 14-58)	
First-Degree Burglary (G.S. 14-51)	
Voluntary Manslaughter (G.S. 14-18)	Class E for offenses before 12/1/1997

Class E

Assault with Deadly Weapon Inflicting Serious Injury (G.S. 14-32(b))	
Assault with Deadly Weapon with Intent to Kill (G.S. 14-32(c))	
Assault with Firearm on a Law Enforcement Officer (G.S. 14-34.5)	
Discharging Weapon into Occupied Property (G.S. 14-34.1(a))	
Second-Degree Kidnapping (G.S. 14-39)	
Second-Degree Sexual Exploitation of a Minor (G.S. 14-190.17)	Class F for offenses before 12/1/2008
Sell/Deliver Controlled Substance within 1,000 Feet of a School (G.S. 90-95(e)(8))	
Sexual Activity by a Substitute Parent or Custodian (G.S. 14-27.31)	Was G.S. 14-27.7(a) before 12/1/2015

Class F

Abduction of Children (G.S. 14-41)	
Assault Inflicting Serious Bodily Injury (G.S. 14-32.4)	
Assault Inflicting Serious Injury on a Law Enforcement Officer (G.S. 14-34.7)	
Assault with Deadly Weapon on Governmental Officer/Employee (G.S. 14-34.2)	
Burning of Certain Other Buildings (G.S. 14-62)	
Failure to Register as a Sex Offender (G.S. 14-208.11)	
Felonious Restraint (G.S. 14-43.3)	
*Habitual Impaired Driving (G.S. 20-138.5)	
Hit and Run Resulting in Serious Bodily Injury or Death (G.S. 20-166(a))	
Indecent Liberties with Children (G.S. 14-202.1)	
Involuntary Manslaughter (G.S. 14-18)	
Malicious Conduct by Prisoner (G.S. 14-258.4)	
Possess or Distribute a Methamphetamine Precursor (G.S. 90-95(d1)(2)	Class H for offenses before 12/1/2004
Possess Weapon of Mass Destruction (G.S. 14-288.8)	
Serious Injury by Vehicle (G.S. 20-141.4(a3))	
Stalking, Second/Subsequent Offense (G.S. 14-277.3A)	Class I for offenses before 3/1/2002

*Special Sentencing rules apply. See **APPENDIX H**, Special Sentencing Rules.

Class G

Child Abuse, Serious Physical Injury/Reckless Disregard for Human Life (G.S. 14-318.4(a5))	Class H for offenses before 12/1/2013
Common Law Robbery (G.S. 14-87.1)	
Forgery/Counterfeiting, Five or More Instruments (G.S. 14-119)	
Identity Theft (G.S. 14-113.20)	
Intimidating a Witness (G.S. 14-226)	Class H for offenses before 12/1/2011
Possession of Firearm by Felon (G.S. 14-415.1)	
Sale of a Schedule I or II Controlled Substance (G.S. 90-95(b)(1))	
Second-Degree Arson (G.S. 14-58)	
Second-Degree Burglary (G.S. 14-51)	
Sexual Activity with a Student by Teacher, etc. (G.S. 14-27.32(a))	Was G.S. 14-27.7(b) before 12/1/2015

Class H

Assault by Strangulation (G.S. 14-32.4(b))	
Breaking or Entering Buildings (G.S. 14-54)	
Carrying Concealed Weapon, Second/Subsequent Offense (G.S. 14-269)	Class I for offenses before 12/1/2014
Cruelty to Animals—Torture, Mutilate, Kill (G.S. 14-360)	Class I for offenses before 12/1/2010
Disclosure of Private Images, Defendant 18 or Older (G.S. 14-190.5A)	
Embezzlement, < $100,000 (G.S. 14-90)	
Felony Larceny (G.S. 14-72)	
Giving/Selling Cell Phone to an Inmate (G.S. 14-258.1)	Class 1 misdemeanor for offenses before 12/1/2014
Habitual Misdemeanor Assault (G.S. 14-33.2)	
Hit and Run Resulting in Injury (G.S. 20-166(a1))	
Indecent Exposure (G.S. 14-190.9(a1))	
Larceny by Employee (G.S. 14-74)	
Manufacture, Deliver, or Possess with Intent to Manufacture, Sell, or Deliver Schedule I or II Controlled Substance (G.S. 90-95(b)(1))	
Obtaining Property by False Pretenses, < $100,000 (G.S. 14-100)	
Possessing Stolen Goods (G.S. 14-71.1)	
Possession of Controlled Substance in Prison/Jail (G.S. 90-95(e)(9))	
Sale of a Schedule III, IV, V, or VI Controlled Substance (G.S. 90-95(b)(2))	
Secretly Peeping, Disseminating Images (G.S. 14-202(h))	
Sex Offender Unlawfully on Premises (G.S. 14-208.18)	
Solicitation of Child by Computer (G.S. 14-202.3)	
Third-Degree Sexual Exploitation of a Minor (G.S. 14-190.17A)	Class I for offenses before 12/1/2008

Class I

Assault on a Firefighter or EMS Technician (G.S. 14-34.6(a))	Class A1 misdemeanor for offenses before 12/1/2011
Breaking into Coin-Operated Machine, Second/Subsequent Offense (G.S. 14-56.1)	
Breaking or Entering Motor Vehicles (G.S. 14-56)	
Counterfeit Controlled Substance; Create, Sell, Deliver, or Possess with Intent to Sell or Deliver (G.S. 90-95(c))	
Crime against Nature (G.S. 14-177)	
Financial Transaction Card Theft (G.S. 14-113.9)	
Forgery of Notes, Checks, Securities (G.S. 14-119(a))	
Indecent Liberties with Student (G.S. 14-202.4)	Class A1 misdemeanor for G.S. 14-202.4(b) for offenses before 12/1/2015
Maintain Dwelling/Motor Vehicle for Controlled Substance, Intentional (G.S. 90-108(a)(7), (b))	
Manufacture, Deliver, or Possess with Intent to Manufacture, Sell, or Deliver Schedule III–VI Controlled Substance (G.S. 90-95(b)(2))	
Obtain a Controlled Substance by Fraud, Intentional (G.S. 90-108(a)(10), (b))	
Possession of Schedule I Controlled Substance (G.S. 90-95(d)(1))	
Preparation to Commit Burglary/Possession of Burglary Tools (G.S. 14-55)	
Safecracking (G.S. 14-89.1)	
*Secretly Peeping, Photographic Images/Devices (G.S. 14-202)	
Sexual Activity with a Student by Non-Teacher, etc. (G.S. 14-27.32(b))	Was Class A1 misdemeanor for offenses before 12/1/2015 under former G.S. 14-27.7(b)
Uttering Forged Paper or Instrument (G.S. 14-120)	
Worthless Check, > $2,000 (G.S. 14-107)	

Note: Offense classifications are subject to change, and different classifications may apply to older offenses.

*Special Sentencing rules apply. *See* APPENDIX H , Special Sentencing Rules.

Appendix B: Offense Class Table for Misdemeanors

Class A1

Assault by Pointing a Gun (G.S. 14-34)

*Assault in Presence of Minor (G.S. 14-33(d))

Assault Inflicting Serious Injury (G.S. 14-33(c)(1))

Assault on Child under 12 Years of Age (G.S. 14-33(c)(3))

Assault on Female (G.S. 14-33(c)(2))

Assault on Government Officer or Employee (G.S. 14-33(c)(4))

Assault on Handicapped Person (G.S. 14-32.1)

Assault on School Employee or Volunteer (G.S. 14-33(c)(6))

Assault with Deadly Weapon (G.S. 14-33(c)(1))

Child Abuse (G.S. 14-318.2)

First-Degree Trespass, Utility Premises or Agricultural Center (G.S. 14-159.12)

Food Stamp Fraud, $100–$500 (G.S. 108A-53.1)

Interfering with Emergency Communication (G.S. 14-286.2)

Misdemeanor Death by Vehicle (G.S. 20-141.1)   Class 1 for offenses before 12/1/2009

Secretly Peeping, Second Offense or with Photo Device (G.S. 14-202)

Sexual Battery (G.S. 14-27.33)   Was G.S. 14-27.5A for offenses before 12/1/2015

*Stalking, First Offense (G.S. 14-277.3A)

Violation of a Valid Protective Order (G.S. 50B-4.1(a))

Class 1

Aggressive Driving (G.S. 20-141.6)

Breaking into Coin-Operated Machine, First Offense (G.S. 14-56.1)

Breaking or Entering Buildings (G.S. 14-54(b))

Communicating Threats (G.S. 14-277.1)

Contributing to the Delinquency of a Juvenile (G.S. 14-316.1)

Cruelty to Animals (G.S. 14-360)

Cyber-Bullying, Defendant 18 or Older (G.S. 14-458.1)

Disclosure of Private Images, Defendant under 18, First Offense (G.S. 14-190.5A)

Domestic Criminal Trespass (G.S. 14-134.3)

Driving While License Revoked (DWI Revocation) (G.S. 20-28(a1))

Escape from Local Confinement Facility (G.S. 14-256)

Escape from Prison, by Misdemeanant (G.S. 148-45)

Failure to Stop for School Bus (G.S. 20-217)

Failure to Yield to Emergency Vehicle, Damage or Injury (G.S. 20-157(h))

False Imprisonment (Common Law)

Forgery (Common Law)

Going Armed to the Terror of the People (Common Law)

Hit-and-Run Property Damage (G.S. 20-166)

Injury to Personal Property, > $200 (G.S. 14-160(b))

Injury to Real Property (G.S. 14-127)

Larceny of Property, Worth $1,000 or Less (G.S. 14-72)

Misrepresentation to Obtain Employment Security Benefits (G.S. 96-18(a))

Misuse of 911 System (G.S. 14-111.4)   Class 3 for offenses before 12/1/2013

Obstruction of Justice (Common Law)

Possession of Certain Schedule II–IV Controlled Substances (G.S. 90-95(d)(2))

Possession of Non-Marijuana Drug Paraphernalia (G.S. 90-113.22)

Possession of Handgun by Minor (G.S. 14-269.7(a))   Class 2 for offenses before 12/1/2011

Possession of over One-Half Ounce of Marijuana (G.S. 90-95(d)(4))

Possession of Stolen Goods (G.S. 14-72)

Possession/Manufacture of Fraudulent ID (G.S. 14-100.1)

Purchase/Possess/Consume Alcohol by Person under 19 (G.S. 18B-302)

*Secretly Peeping (G.S. 14-202)

*Shoplifting/Concealment of Merchandise, Third Offense in 5 Years (G.S. 14-72.1)

Solicitation of Prostitution, First Offense (G.S. 14-205.1)   Was G.S. 14-204 for offenses before 10/1/2013

Speeding to Elude (G.S. 20-141.5)

Tax Return Violations (G.S. 105-236)

Unauthorized Use of a Motor Vehicle (G.S. 14-72.2)

Use of Red or Blue Light (G.S. 20-130.1)

Weapon (Non-Firearm or Explosive) on School Property (G.S. 14-269.2)

*Worthless Check, Closed Account (G.S. 14-107(d)(4))

*Worthless Check, Fourth Conviction (G.S. 14-107(d)(1))

---

*Special Sentencing rules apply. *See* **APPENDIX H** , Special Sentencing Rules.

Class 2

Carrying Concealed Weapons, First Offense (G.S. 14-269(a), (a1))

Cyber-Bullying, Defendant under 18 (G.S. 14-458.1)

Cyberstalking (G.S. 14-196.3)

Defrauding Innkeeper (G.S. 14-110)

Disorderly Conduct (G.S. 14-288.4)

Driving after Consuming (G.S. 20-138.3)

Failure to Appear on a Misdemeanor (G.S. 15A-543)

Failure to Report Accident (G.S. 20-166.1)

Failure to Work after Being Paid (G.S. 14-104)

Failure to Yield to Emergency Vehicle (G.S. 20-157)

False Report to Police (G.S. 14-225)

Financial Card Fraud (G.S. 14-113.13)

First-Degree Trespass (G.S. 14-159.12)

Furnishing False Information to Officer (G.S. 20-29)

Gambling (G.S. 14-292)

Harassing Phone Calls (G.S. 14-196)

Indecent Exposure (G.S. 14-190.9)

Injury to Personal Property, $200 or Less (G.S. 14-160(a))

Marine/Wildlife Violations, Second/Subsequent Offense (G.S. 113-135)

Possession of Schedule V Controlled Substance (G.S. 90-95(d)(3))

Racing/Speed Competition (G.S. 20-141.3)

Reckless Driving to Endanger (G.S. 20-140)

Resisting Officers (G.S. 14-223)

*Shoplifting/Concealment of Merchandise, Second Offense in 3 Years (G.S. 14-72.1)

Simple Assault/Assault and Battery/Affray (G.S. 14-33(a))

Standing/Sitting/Lying on Highway (G.S. 20-174.1)

Class 3

Allowing Unlicensed Person to Drive (G.S. 20-34)

Conversion by Bailee, Lessee, etc. ($400 or less) (G.S. 14-168.1)

Driving a Commercial Vehicle after Consuming Alcohol (G.S. 20-138.2A)

Driving While License Revoked (Non-DWI Revocation) (G.S. 20-28(a))

Expired, Altered, or Revoked Registration/Tag (G.S. 20-111(2))

Failure to Comply with License Restrictions (G.S. 20-7(e))

Failure to Return Hired Property (G.S. 14-167)

Failure to Return Rented Property (G.S. 14-168.4)

Fictitious/Altered Title/Registration (G.S. 20-111(2))

Intoxicated and Disruptive in Public (G.S. 14-444)

*Littering, 15 Pounds or Less, Non-Commercial (G.S. 14-399(c))

Local Ordinance Violation (G.S. 14-4)

Marine/Wildlife Violations, First Offense (G.S. 113-135)

No Operator's License (G.S. 20-7(a))

Obtaining Property for Worthless Check (G.S. 14-106)

Open Container, First Offense (G.S. 20-138.7)

Operating Unregistered Vehicle or Not Displaying Plate (G.S. 20-111(1))

Operating Vehicle without Insurance (G.S. 20-313(a))

*Possession of Marijuana (One-Half Ounce or Less) (G.S. 90-95(a)(3))

Possession of Marijuana Drug Paraphernalia (G.S. 90-113.22A)

Purchase/Possess/Consume Alcohol by 19 or 20 Year Old (G.S. 18B-302(i))

Second-Degree Trespass (G.S. 14-159.13)

*Shoplifting/Concealment of Merchandise, First Offense (G.S. 14-72.1)

Speeding, More Than 15 m.p.h. over Limit or over 80 m.p.h. (G.S. 20-141(j1))

Unsealed Wine/Liquor in Passenger Area (G.S. 18B-401)

Window Tinting Violation (G.S. 20-127)

*Worthless Check (Simple, $2,000 or Less) (G.S. 14-107(d)(1))

Selected Infractions

Failure to Carry/Sign Registration Card (G.S. 20-57(c), 20-176(a1))

Failure to Carry License (G.S. 20-7(a))

Failure to Notify DMV of Address Change for License (G.S. 20-7.1) or Registration (G.S. 20-67)

Fishing without a License (G.S. 113-174.1(a) and -270.1B(a))

Operating a Motor Vehicle with Expired License (G.S. 20-7(f))

Ramp Meter Violation (G.S. 20-158(c)(6))

Violations of Boating and Water Safety Provisions of Art. 1, G.S. Ch. 75A, Except as Otherwise Provided

---

Note: Offense classifications are subject to change, and different classifications may apply to older offenses.

*Special Sentencing rules apply. *See* **APPENDIX H**, Special Sentencing Rules.

Appendix C: Aggravating Factors (G.S. 15A-1340.16(d))

1. The defendant induced others to participate in the commission of the offense or occupied a position of leadership or dominance of other participants.
2. The defendant joined with more than one other person in committing the offense and was not charged with committing a conspiracy.
2a. The offense was committed for the benefit of, or at the direction of, any criminal gang, with the specific intent to promote, further, or assist in any criminal conduct by gang members, and the defendant was not charged with committing a conspiracy.
3. The offense was committed for the purpose of avoiding or preventing a lawful arrest or effecting an escape from custody.
4. The defendant was hired or paid to commit the offense.
5. The offense was committed to disrupt or hinder the lawful exercise of any governmental function or the enforcement of laws.
6. The offense was committed against or proximately caused serious injury to a present or former law enforcement officer, employee of the Division of Adult Correction and Juvenile Justice (DACJJ) of the Department of Public Safety, jailer, fireman, emergency medical technician, ambulance attendant, social worker, justice or judge, clerk or assistant or deputy clerk of court, magistrate, prosecutor, juror, or witness against the defendant, while engaged in the performance of that person's official duties or because of the exercise of that person's official duties.
6a. The offense was committed against or proximately caused serious harm as defined in G.S. 14-163.1 or death to a law enforcement agency animal, an assistance animal, or a search and rescue animal as defined in G.S. 14-163.1, while engaged in the performance of the animal's official duties. [*Offenses committed on/after 12/1/2009.*]
7. The offense was especially heinous, atrocious, or cruel.
8. The defendant knowingly created a great risk of death to more than one person by means of a weapon or device which would normally be hazardous to the lives of more than one person.
9. The defendant held public elected or appointed office or public employment at the time of the offense and the offense directly related to the conduct of the office or employment.
9a. The defendant is a firefighter or rescue squad worker, and the offense is directly related to service as a firefighter or rescue squad worker. [*Offenses committed on/after 12/1/2013.*]
10. The defendant was armed with or used a deadly weapon at the time of the crime.
11. The victim was very young, or very old, or mentally or physically infirm, or handicapped.
12. The defendant committed the offense while on pretrial release on another charge.
12a. The defendant has, during the ten-year period prior to the commission of the offense for which the defendant is being sentenced, been found by a court of this State to be in willful violation of the conditions of probation imposed pursuant to a suspended sentence or been found by the Post-Release Supervision and Parole Commission to be in willful violation of a condition of parole or post-release supervision imposed pursuant to release from incarceration. [*Offenses committed on/after 12/1/2008.*]
13. The defendant involved a person under the age of 16 in the commission of the crime.
13a. The defendant committed an offense and knew or reasonably should have known that a person under the age of 18 who was not involved in the commission of the offense was in a position to see or hear the offense. [*Offenses committed on/after 12/1/2015.*]
14. The offense involved an attempted or actual taking of property of great monetary value or damage causing great monetary loss, or the offense involved an unusually large quantity of contraband.
15. The defendant took advantage of a position of trust or confidence, including a domestic relationship, to commit the offense.
16. The offense involved the sale or delivery of a controlled substance to a minor.
16a. The offense is the manufacture of methamphetamine and was committed where a person under the age of 18 lives, was present, or was otherwise endangered by exposure to the drug, its ingredients, its by-products, or its waste.
16b. The offense is the manufacture of methamphetamine and was committed in a dwelling that is one of four or more contiguous dwellings.
17. The offense for which the defendant stands convicted was committed against a victim because of the victim's race, color, religion, nationality, or country of origin.
18. The defendant does not support the defendant's family.
18a. The defendant has previously been adjudicated delinquent for an offense that would be a Class A, B1, B2, C, D, or E felony if committed by an adult.
19. The serious injury inflicted upon the victim is permanent and debilitating.
19a. The offense is a violation of G.S. 14-43.11 (human trafficking), G.S. 14-43.12 (involuntary servitude), or G.S. 14-43.13 (sexual servitude) and involved multiple victims. [*Offenses committed on/after 10/1/2013.*]
19b. The offense is a violation of G.S. 14-43.11 (human trafficking), G.S. 14-43.12 (involuntary servitude), or G.S. 14-43.13 (sexual servitude), and the victim suffered serious injury as a result of the offense. [*Offenses committed on/after 10/1/2013.*]
20. Any other aggravating factor reasonably related to the purposes of sentencing.

Note: The numbering of the aggravating and mitigating factors in this handbook mirrors the numbering used in the referenced General Statutes sections.

Appendix D: Mitigating Factors (G.S. 15A-1340.16(e))

1. The defendant committed the offense under duress, coercion, threat, or compulsion that was insufficient to constitute a defense but significantly reduced the defendant's culpability.

2. The defendant was a passive participant or played a minor role in the commission of the offense.

3. The defendant was suffering from a mental or physical condition that was insufficient to constitute a defense but significantly reduced the defendant's culpability for the offense.

4. The defendant's age, immaturity, or limited mental capacity at the time of commission of the offense significantly reduced the defendant's culpability for the offense.

5. The defendant has made substantial or full restitution to the victim.

6. The victim was more than 16 years of age and was a voluntary participant in the defendant's conduct or consented to it.

7. The defendant aided in the apprehension of another felon or testified truthfully on behalf of the prosecution in another prosecution of a felony.

8. The defendant acted under strong provocation, or the relationship between the defendant and the victim was otherwise extenuating.

9. The defendant could not reasonably foresee that the defendant's conduct would cause or threaten serious bodily harm or fear, or the defendant exercised caution to avoid such consequences.

10. The defendant reasonably believed that the defendant's conduct was legal.

11. Prior to arrest or at an early stage of the criminal process, the defendant voluntarily acknowledged wrongdoing in connection with the offense to a law enforcement officer.

12. The defendant has been a person of good character or has had a good reputation in the community in which the defendant lives.

13. The defendant is a minor and has reliable supervision available.

14. The defendant has been honorably discharged from the Armed Forces of the United States.

15. The defendant has accepted responsibility for the defendant's criminal conduct.

16. The defendant has entered and is currently involved in or has successfully completed a drug treatment program or an alcohol treatment program subsequent to arrest and prior to trial.

17. The defendant supports the defendant's family.

18. The defendant has a support system in the community.

19. The defendant has a positive employment history or is gainfully employed.

20. The defendant has a good treatment prognosis, and a workable treatment plan is available.

21. Any other mitigating factor reasonably related to the purposes of sentences.

Appendix E: Crimes Covered under the Crime Victims' Rights Act (CVRA) (G.S. 15A-830)

Felonies

- Any Class A through E felony.
- Abduction of children (G.S. 14-41).
- Assault inflicting serious bodily injury (G.S. 14-32.4).
- Assault on a handicapped person (G.S. 14-32.1(e)).
- Assault on an executive, legislative, or court official with a deadly weapon or inflicting serious injury (G.S. 14-16.6(b)–(c)).
- Assault on emergency personnel with a dangerous weapon or substance (G.S. 14-288.9).
- Assault with a firearm or deadly weapon on a government officer/employee or campus/company police officer (G.S. 14-34.2).
- Assault with a firearm, deadly weapon, or inflicting serious bodily injury on a firefighter, emergency medical technician, or emergency room nurse or physician (G.S. 14-34.6(b)–(c)).
- Common-law robbery (G.S. 14-87.1).
- Domestic abuse or neglect of a disabled or elder adult causing injury or serious injury (G.S. 14-32.3(a)–(b)).
- Felonious restraint (G.S. 14-43.3).
- Habitual impaired driving (G.S. 20-138.5).
- Habitual misdemeanor assault (G.S. 14-33.2).
- Human trafficking of adults (G.S. 14-43.11).
- Involuntary manslaughter (G.S. 14-18).
- Participating in the prostitution of a minor (former G.S. 14-190.19).
- Patient abuse/neglect causing serious bodily injury (G.S. 14-32.2(b)(3)).
- Second-degree arson (G.S. 14-58).
- Second-degree burglary (G.S. 14-51).
- Stalking, second or subsequent offense or when a court order is in effect (G.S. 14-277.3A or former G.S. 14-277.3).
- Taking indecent liberties with children (G.S. 14-202.1).
- Third-degree sexual exploitation of a minor (G.S. 14-190.17A).
- Any attempt of the felonies listed above if the attempt is punishable as a felony.

Misdemeanors

The following apply only when the offense is committed between persons who have a personal relationship as defined in G.S. 50B-1(b). These include: current/former spouse; persons of opposite sex who live or have lived together or who are in or were in a dating relationship; parents/children; grandparents/grandchildren; child in common; current or former household members.

- Assault by pointing a gun (G.S. 14-34).
- Assault inflicting serious injury or using a deadly weapon (G.S. 14-33(c)(1)).
- Assault on a female (G.S. 14-33(c)(2)).
- Domestic criminal trespass (G.S. 14-134.3).
- Simple assault or affray (G.S. 14-33(a)).
- Stalking, first offense (G.S. 14-277.3A or former G.S. 14-277.3).

Protective Order Violations

- Any violation of a valid protective order under G.S. 50B-4.1.

Appendix F: Crimes Requiring Sex Offender Registration (G.S. 14-208.6)

Sexually Violent Offenses (G.S. 14-208.6(5))

First-Degree Forcible Rape (G.S. 14-27.21)	Committed on/after 12/1/2015
Second-Degree Forcible Rape (G.S. 14-27.22)	Committed on/after 12/1/2015
Statutory Rape of a Child by an Adult (G.S. 14-27.23)	Committed on/after 12/1/2015
First-Degree Statutory Rape (G.S. 14-27.24)	Effective 12/1/2015
Statutory Rape of Person ≤ 15yo/D 6+ Years Older (G.S. 14-27.25(a))	Committed on/after 12/1/2015
First-Degree Forcible Sexual Offense (G.S. 14-27.26)	Committed on/after 12/1/2015
Second-Degree Forcible Sexual Offense (G.S. 14-27.27)	Committed on/after 12/1/2015
Statutory Sexual Offense with a Child by an Adult (G.S. 14-27.28)	Committed on/after 12/1/2015
First-Degree Statutory Sexual Offense (G.S. 14-27.29)	Committed on/after 12/1/2015
Statutory Sexual Offense with Person ≤ 15yo/D 6+ Years Older (G.S. 14-27.30(a))	Committed on/after 12/1/2015
Sexual Activity by a Substitute Parent or Custodian (G.S. 14-27.31)	Committed on/after 12/1/2015
Sexual Activity with a Student (G.S. 14-27.32)	Committed on/after 12/1/2015
Sexual Battery (G.S. 14-27.33)	Committed on/after 12/1/2015
Human Trafficking (*Only if Victim < 18 or for Sex Servitude*) (G.S. 14-43.11)	Committed on/after 12/1/2013
Sexual Servitude (G.S. 14-43.13)	Committed on/after 12/1/2006
Incest between Near Relatives (G.S. 14-178)	Convicted/released from prison on/after 1/1/1996
Employ Minor in Offense/Public Morality (G.S. 14-190.6)	Convicted/released from prison on/after 1/1/1996
Felony Indecent Exposure (G.S. 14-190.9(a1))	Committed on/after 12/1/2005
First-Degree Sexual Exploitation of Minor (G.S. 14-190.16)	Convicted/released from prison on/after 1/1/1996
Second-Degree Sexual Exploitation of Minor (G.S. 14-190.17)	Convicted/released from prison on/after 1/1/1996
Third-Degree Sexual Exploitation of Minor (G.S. 14-190.17A)	Convicted/released from prison on/after 1/1/1996
Taking Indecent Liberties with Children (G.S. 14-202.1)	Convicted/released from prison on/after 1/1/1996
Solicitation of Child by Computer (G.S. 14-202.3)	Committed on/after 12/1/2005
Taking Indecent Liberties with a Student (G.S. 14-202.4(a))	Convicted/released from prison on/after 12/1/2009
Patronizing Minor/Mentally Disabled Prostitute (G.S. 14-205.2(c)–(d))	Committed on/after 10/1/2013
Prostitution of Minor/Mentally Disabled Child (G.S. 14-205.3(b))	Committed on/after 10/1/2013
Parent/Caretaker Prostitution (G.S. 14-318.4(a1))	Convicted/released from prison on/after 12/1/2008
Parent/Guardian Commit/Allow Sexual Act (G.S. 14-318.4(a2))	Convicted/released from prison on/after 12/1/2008
Former First-Degree Rape (G.S. 14-27.2)	Convicted/released from prison on/after 1/1/1996
Former Rape of a Child by an Adult Offender (G.S. 14-27.2A)	Committed on/after 12/1/2008
Former Second-Degree Rape (G.S. 14-27.3)	Convicted/released from prison on/after 1/1/1996
Former First-Degree Sexual Offense (G.S. 14-27.4)	Convicted/released from prison on/after 1/1/1996
Former Sexual Offense with a Child by an Adult Offender (G.S. 14-27.4A)	Committed on/after 12/1/2008
Former Second-Degree Sexual Offense (G.S. 14-27.5)	Convicted/released from prison on/after 1/1/1996
Former Sexual Battery (G.S. 14-27.5A)	Committed on/after 12/1/2005
Former Attempted Rape/Sexual Offense (G.S. 14-27.6)	Convicted/released from prison on/after 1/1/1996
Former Intercourse/Sexual Offense w/Certain Victims (G.S. 14-27.7)	Convicted/released from prison on/after 1/1/1996
Former Statutory Rape/Sexual Offense (13–15yo/D 6+ Years Older) (G.S. 14-27.7A(a))	Committed on/after 12/1/2006
Former Promoting Prostitution of Minor (G.S. 14-190.18)	Convicted/released from prison on/after 1/1/1996
Former Participating in Prostitution of Minor (G.S. 14-190.19)	Convicted/released from prison on/after 1/1/1996

Offenses Against a Minor (G.S. 14-208.6(1m))—Reportable Only When Victim Is a Minor and the Offender Is Not the Minor's Parent

Kidnapping (G.S. 14-39)	Committed on/after 4/1/1998 (at a minimum)
Abduction of Children (G.S. 14-41)	Committed on/after 4/1/1998 (at a minimum)
Felonious Restraint (G.S. 14-43.3)	Committed on/after 4/1/1998 (at a minimum)

Peeping Crimes (G.S. 14-208.6(4)d.)—Reportable Only if the Court Decides That Registration Furthers Purposes of the Registry and That the Offender Is a Danger to Community

Felony Peeping under G.S. 14-202(d), (e), (f), (g), or (h)	Committed on/after 12/1/2003
or Second/Subsequent Conviction of:	
Misdemeanor Peeping under G.S. 14-202(a) or (c)	Committed on/after 12/1/2003
Misdemeanor Peeping w/Mirror/Device under G.S. 14-202(a1)	Committed on/after 12/1/2004

Sale of a Child (G.S. 14-208.6(4)e.). Reportable only if the sentencing court rules under G.S. 14-43.14(e) that the person is a danger to the community and required to register. (*Offenses committed on/after 12/1/2012*.)

Attempt. Final convictions for attempts to commit an "offense against a minor" or a "sexually violent offense" are reportable. G.S. 14-208.6(4)a. (*Offenses committed on/after 4/1/1998*, at a minimum, unless target offense has later effective date.)

Conspiracy/Solicitation. Conspiracy and solicitation to commit an "offense against a minor" or a "sexually violent offense" are reportable. G.S. 14-208.6(1m); -208.6(5). (*Offenses committed on/after 12/1/1999*, unless underlying offense has a later effective date.)

Aiding and Abetting. Aiding and abetting an "offense against a minor" or "sexually violent offense" is reportable only if the court finds that registration furthers the purposes of the registry (set out in G.S. 14-208.5). G.S. 14-208.6(4)a. (*Offenses committed on/after 12/1/1999*, unless underlying offense has a later effective date.)

Appendix G: Place of Confinement Chart

	Felony G.S. 15A-1352(b)	Misdemeanor G.S. 15A-1352(a)	Driving While Impaired (DWI) G.S. 15A-1352(f)
Active	Division of Adult Correction and Juvenile Justice (DACJJ)	*Sentences imposed on/after 10/1/2014:* ≤ 90 days: Local jail > 90 days: Statewide Misdemeanant Confinement Program (SMCP) *Sentences imposed before 10/1/2014:* ≤ 90 days: Local jail 91–180 days: SMCP > 180 days: DACJJ	*Sentences imposed on/after 1/1/2015:* SMCP, regardless of sentence length *Sentences imposed before 1/1/2015 (G.S. 20-176(c1)):* • Defendants with no prior DWI or jail imprisonment for a Ch. 20 offense: Local jail • Defendants with a prior DWI or prior jail imprisonment for a Ch. 20 offense: ≤ 90 days: Local jail 91–180 days: Local jail or DACJJ, in court's discretion > 180 days: DACJJ
Split Sentence at Sentencing G.S. 15A-1351(a)	*Continuous:* Local jail or DACJJ *Noncontinuous:* Local jail or treatment facility	Local jail or treatment facility	Local jail or treatment facility
Split Sentence as a Modification of Probation G.S. 15A-1344(e)	*Continuous:* Local jail or DACJJ *Noncontinuous:* Local jail or treatment facility	*Continuous:* Local jail or DACJJ *Noncontinuous:* Local jail or treatment facility	*Continuous:* Local jail or DACJJ *Noncontinuous:* Local jail or treatment facility
Confinement in Response to Violation (CRV) G.S. 15A-1344(d2)	DACJJ	Place of confinement indicated in the judgment suspending sentence	Place of confinement indicated in the judgment suspending sentence
Quick Dip G.S. 15A-1343(a1)(3) and -1343.2	Local jail	Local jail	N/A
Nonpayment of Fine G.S. 15A-1352	DACJJ	Local jail	N/A
Probation Revocation	Place of confinement indicated in the judgment suspending sentence	Place of confinement indicated in the judgment suspending sentence	Place of confinement indicated in the judgment suspending sentence

Notes

Work release. Notwithstanding any other provision of law, the court may order that a consenting misdemeanant (including DWI) be granted work release. The court may commit the defendant to a particular prison or jail facility in the county or to a jail in another county to facilitate the work release arrangement. If the commitment is to a jail in another county, the sentencing court must first get the consent of the sheriff or board of commissioners there. G.S. 15A-1352(d).

Overcrowded confinement. When a jail is overcrowded or otherwise unable to accommodate additional prisoners, inmates may be transferred to another jail or, in certain circumstances, to DACJJ, as provided in G.S. 148-32.1(b). A judge also has authority to sentence an inmate to the jail of an adjacent county when the local jail is unfit or insecure, G.S. 162-38, or has been destroyed by fire or other accident, G.S. 162-40.

Apppendix H: Special Sentencing Rules

The listed crimes are a selection of commonly charged offenses that are sentenced under Structured Sentencing, but with the additional rules or exceptions indicated below. The list is not comprehensive.

Statutory Rape of a Child by an Adult (G.S. 14-27.23), and Statutory Sexual Offense with a Child by an Adult (G.S. 14-27.28)

Mandatory minimum sentence of no less than 300 months and mandatory lifetime satellite-based monitoring upon release from prison. The statutes also provide for a sentence of up to life without parole with judicial findings of "egregious aggravation," but that provision has been ruled unconstitutional. State v. Singletary, 786 S.E.2d 712 (2016) (N.C. Ct. App. 2016).

Assault in the Presence of a Minor on a Person with Whom the Defendant Has a Personal Relationship (G.S. 14-33(d))

A defendant sentenced to Community punishment must be placed on supervised probation. A defendant sentenced for a second or subsequent offense must be sentenced to an active punishment of no less than 30 days.

Concealment of Merchandise (Shoplifting) (G.S. 14-72.1)

First offense. Any term of imprisonment may be suspended only on condition that the defendant complete at least 24 hours of community service.

Second offense within three years of conviction. Any term of imprisonment may be suspended only on condition that the defendant serve a split sentence of at least 72 hours, complete at least 72 hours of community service, or both.

Third or subsequent offense within five years of conviction of two other offenses. Any term of imprisonment may be suspended only on condition that the defendant serve a split sentence of at least 11 days.

If the sentencing judge finds that the defendant is unable to perform community service, the judge may pronounce a sentence that he or she deems appropriate. If the judge imposes an active sentence, he or she may not give jail credit for the first 24 hours of pretrial confinement.

Worthless Checks (G.S. 14-107)

If the court imposes any sentence other than an active sentence, it may require the payment of restitution to the victim for the amount of the check, any service charges imposed by the bank, and any processing fees imposed by the payee, and it must impose witness fees for each prosecuting witness.

Fourth and subsequent offenses. The court must, as a condition of probation, order the defendant not to maintain a checking account or make or utter a check for three years.

Secretly Peeping (G.S. 14-202)

Any probation for a first-time offender may include a requirement that the defendant obtain a psychological evaluation and comply with any recommended treatment. Probation for a second or subsequent offense must include that requirement.

Falsely Representing Self as Law Enforcement Officer (G.S. 14-277)

Intermediate punishment is always authorized for this crime.

Stalking (G.S. 14-277.3A)

A defendant sentenced to Community punishment must be placed on supervised probation.

Littering (15 Pounds or Less, Non-Commercial) (G.S. 14-399(c))

Punishable by a fine from $250 to $1,000. The court may also require 8 to 24 hours of community service, which shall entail picking up litter, if feasible.

Sell or Give Alcoholic Beverage to Person Under 21 (G.S. 18B-302; -302.1)

If the court imposes a non-active sentence, it must impose a fine of at least $250 and at least 25 hours of community service.

Subsequent offense within four years of conviction. If the court imposes a non-active sentence, it must impose a fine of at least $500 and at least 150 hours of community service.

Aiding or Abetting a Violation of G.S. 18B-302 by a Person Over the Lawful Age (G.S. 18B-302.1)

If the court imposes a non-active sentence, it must impose a fine of at least $500 and at least 25 hours of community service.

Subsequent offense within four years of conviction. If the court imposes a non-active sentence, it must impose a fine of at least $1,000 and at least 150 hours of community service.

Habitual Impaired Driving (G.S. 20-138.5)

Mandatory minimum sentence of no less than 12 months, which shall not be suspended. Sentences shall run consecutively with any sentence being served.

Felony Death by Vehicle (G.S. 20-141.4(a1))

Intermediate punishment is authorized for Prior Record Level I defendants.

Aggravated Felony Death by Vehicle (G.S. 20-141.4(a5))

The court must sentence the defendant from the aggravated range, without the need for any findings of aggravating factors.

Possession of Up to One-Half Ounce of Marijuana or One-Twentieth of an Ounce of Hashish (G.S. 90-95(d)(4))

Any sentence of imprisonment must be suspended, and the judge may not impose a split sentence at sentencing.

Notes

Notes